Netted Beadwork

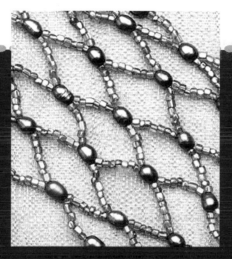

Diane Fitzgerald

INTERWEAVE PRESS
www.interweave.com

Editor: Judith Durant
Technical editor: Dorothy T. Ratigan
Original illustrations: Diane Fitzgerald
Final illustrations: Gayle Ford
Photography: Joe Coca
Photostyling: Ann Swanson
Cover and interior design: Karen Schober
Production: Dean Howes
Proofreaders: Nancy Arndt, Melanie Aswell

Interweave Press, Inc.
201 East Fourth Street
Loveland, CO 80537-5655 USA
www.interweave.com

Printed in China by Everbest

Library of Congress Cataloging-in-Publication Data

Fitzgerald, Diane.
  Beadwork how-to : netted beadwork / Diane Fitzgerald.
     p. cm. — (Beadwork how-to)
  ISBN 1-931499-15-2
  1. Beadwork. 2. Netting. I. Title: Netted beadwork. II. Title. III. Beadwork how-to book
  TT860.F58 2003
  745.58'2—dc21
                          2003001528

10 9 8 7 6 5 4 3 2 1

Dedication

This book is dedicated to my husband, Alan Shilepsky, who is always there to help but never interferes in the pursuit of my passion.

Thank You's

My heartiest thanks for all their help go to: Judith Durant, a trusted editor, Dot Ratigan for her careful review of the instructions; Mariane Petersen, Greenland National Museum and Archives, Nuuk, Greenland for a book about the national costume of netted collars with instructions; Lydia Borin, the Bead Wrangler, for donating a piece of Gudjarat beadwork and for her encouragement; Carole Morris for use of her photographs; and Carol Perrenoud and Virginia Blakelock for sharing their knowledge and photographs of their work.

Roxanne Thoeny

contents

introduction

My goal in writing this book is to offer a fresh look at netted beadwork and all its potential. I envisioned projects that would be wearable (stylish and contemporary), doable, and beautiful. Realizing that few people have the luxury, the stamina, or the inclination to do huge complex projects that involve many months of work, I've included instructions for small components, such as the Pom-pom Flowers and Triangles, which give quick satisfaction and can be combined to create more impressive pieces. I also present projects that beaders can wear to work in a variety of jobs where they can share their enjoyment of beads and show off their skills. Nothing encourages us more than admiration.

First row, left to right: Ann Gilbert, Jane Langenback, Diane Fitzgerald, and Roxanne Thoeny; second row: Elizabeth Ofstead, Carla Abler-Erickson, Rose Hamerlinck, Doris Coghill, and Bonnie Voelker.

I also wanted a book that would inspire beaders with its rich variety. Knowing that I could never produce such variety myself, I put a call out to a group of students who have taken classes from me for several years. I warned them that this would be an intensive class and if they signed on, they would be expected to test instructions and produce variations of the projects I proposed. Eight people rose to the challenge! There was a healthy bit of competition that spurred them on and made each class almost like opening presents at Christmas as each student showed what they had made. The oohs and ahs around the table as we took turns showing our progress were spontaneous and excited. Each person came through in her own unique and sometimes unexpected way. I have the highest degree of respect for the participants, their talents, and their accomplishments. My heartfelt thanks go to the loyal group of beaders who made writing this book so much fun: Carla Abler, Doris Coghill, Ann Gilbert, Rose Hamerlinck, Jane Langenback, Liz Ofstead, Roxanne Thoeny, and Bonnie Voelker.

Netted Beadwork Around the World

Of all beadwork types, netting may be the most broadly used method of beadwork and is surely among the oldest. Let us begin our survey with one of the most beautiful pieces of netting I've seen, which was made about a hundred years ago.

Straits Chinese Beadwork

In sheer beauty of color and design, no beadwork surpasses the work of the Straits Chinese in the late nineteenth century. With jewel-like colors and ornate designs, they depicted peonies, roses, butterflies, lotus flowers, phoenix, and other exotic birds in fabulous bordered and fringed panels for a bridal couple's wedding chamber and for household items. Often using three-bead netting, these designs were painstakingly executed with utmost care. Pieces adorned the canopy of a four-poster bed, the washstand and mirror, small tables and stools, and tassels hung from doorways and windows. The result was a sumptuous feast for the eyes to excite and inspire the newly married husband and wife as they enjoyed an elaborate twelve-day ceremony.

These designs reflect the rich Chinese culture brought to Malaysia by the Southern Chinese as they settled in Singapore, Penang, and along the Straits of Malacca. As the British colonized the area, these Chinese established themselves as merchants and property owners and through hard work accumulated their fortunes. This culture, and its arts and crafts, are now nearly lost and only tangible mementos, such as beadwork, endure.

The beadwork was purely ornamental, primarily adorning household furnishings. Although rarely used as jewelry, lavishly beaded slippers, collars, belts, and purses were worn. The beadwork had no spiritual, magical, or religious significance, and it was enjoyed at weddings but never appeared at funerals.

The Straits Chinese used beads primarily from Europe, namely Italy, Bohemia, and France. Most beadwork was done with beads about .75 to 1 mm in diameter but some were as small as .5 mm. Both glass beads— sometimes the single-faceted charlottes (also referred to as one-cuts) which give a subtle sparkle—and metal beads of brass and steel were used. These beads were purchased on short hanks, then placed in small, shallow porcelain dishes for pick up.

LEFT: Fringed Pouch. Identical panels adorn both sides of this 13" × 9" (including fringe) bag. Note the characteristic fringe design and color. The size 15° charlottes give the piece subtle highlights. The floral motif is worked in the following colors: center flower is mustard opaque, cobalt opaque, greasy turquoise, and turquoise opaque; side flowers are red whitehearts, transparent cranberry, and rose opaque; leaves are opaque green and transparent dark green; branches are dark transparent amethyst; background is pale gray opalescent; fringe is black, white, and other colors used in the panels. Collection of Blakelock and Perrenoud.

FAR RIGHT: Identical panels adorn both sides.

This little reminiscence by Ho Wing Meng
will give you the flavor of buying beadwork and other notions
a hundred years ago in Singapore.

"I remember well that my mother and aunts used to purchase all their supplies of colourful silk and cotton threads, balls of woollen threads for knitting, needles, tapes, laces, cotton gauze, buttons, beads, sequins, velvets and tambour frames of various sizes from the jarong-man who always went about peddling his three-wheeled vehicle. He usually wore a blue or black silk garment consisting of a loose, long-sleeved tunic with silken fasteners and a pair of baggy pants. Over his head, he wore a broad-brimmed, peasant hat that spread beyond his shoulders to protect him from the fierce heat of the tropics. His feet were shod with black velvet shoes. And whenever mother needed a fresh supply of threads, needles, buttons and beads, she would tell us to hail the jarong-man, and one of us would rush out into the street yelling, 'Jarong!' at the top of his voice several times. He would invariably arrive a few minutes later, eager to show us his range of goods.

"Inside each of those little drawers built into the front and sides of a big wooden cabinet mounted on his tricycle he carried a fascinating assortment of colourful things. There were boxes upon boxes of buttons of every shape, colour and design; twirls of silk threads with their characteristic sheen and brilliant colours; balls of thick woollen threads; piles of delicate white laces with intricate designs; sheets of velvets of deep colours and fine texture; needles of all sizes; Chinese cloth buttons or fasteners of beautiful designs; beads and sequins of incredible beauty and so on. The jarong-man always attracted a small crowd of wide-eyed children who came to gasp at the beautiful things he sold to their mothers."

EXCERPTED FROM *STRAITS CHINESE BEADWORK AND EMBROIDERY: A COLLECTOR'S GUIDE* BY HO WING MENG, PP. 40–41.

Gujarat Beadwork

There is a liveliness and folkloric quality about the netted beadwork done in Gujarat State in northwestern India. Like that of the Straits Chinese, this beadwork is closely related to the embroidery that adorned home and furnishings, brightening and enriching daily life for those with the patience to produce it or the money to purchase it. The motifs are often set against a white background and are surrounded by a narrow geometric border. They represent animals, people, plants, and inanimate objects such as wagons. In some very old examples, deities are depicted. Human figures are often shown in a frontal position, women in activities such as churning or rocking a cradle, while men are shown driving animals or carts. These figures may represent characters from folk tales.

A toran, or hanging for a doorway, made in Gujarat, India. Collection of the author.

Among the animals depicted, elephants are the most popular. They are shown decorated with tapestries and their trunks are brightly painted. Other animals such as buffalo, cows, horses, fierce lions, playful monkeys, dogs with upturned tails, cats, and camels were also added to relieve the tedium of working a large plain white area. Colorful peacocks were also frequently used, sometimes with tails fanned out and sometimes with tails trailing behind the bird. Often the peacock is shown with a purple neck and green, yellow, and red blended in the body and tail. Other popular birds included parakeets, swans, ducks, and chickens.

Pieces of netted beadwork were used in many ways. Square pieces, about eighteen to twenty-four inches in size, and occasionally hexagon-shaped pieces, were used as table covers; rectangles and round shapes served as pillow covers; and elongated pieces were used at the top of a wall where it joins the ceiling, just as in the United States we use wallpaper borders. Netted beadwork was also used in fan covers, hammocks, and to cover knickknacks. Pieces with tabular shapes suspended from them were hung over doorways.

American and European Beadwork

Although the Victorians were prolific beadworkers, the broad netted collars seen in so many cultures were shown less frequently here. In England, France, and other parts of Europe in the late nineteenth century, netting was used for purses, belts, lamp fringes, ornaments, and as a connecting stitch in *passe-menterie*. In the 1920s and 1930s, an immensely popular necklace consisting of a very long narrow band of netting ending with loops of seed beads and occasionally accent beads was worn. The style looked good with the low-waisted slim-cut flapper dresses, and the necklace bounced and swayed as the wearer danced the Charleston. In the 1940s and 1950s, small netted collars often made with pearls were popular and worn with sweaters.

Two Victorian-era women wearing netted beadwork. At left, a graceful band of netting drapes from the shoulders of a dress. Bottom, a netted necklace is worn with a ruffled lace collar and a metal chain. Photos collection of the author.

"Flapper" necklaces from the 1920s and 1930s were worn with low-waisted chemise-style dresses accenting the willowy silhouette popular in that era. Collection of the author.

A lacy ruffled collar of beads softens the look of this plaid dress. Photo collection of the author.

Pearl Collar. A typical collar worn with a sweater by "bobby-soxers" in the 1940s. Collection of the author.

A small netted purse with string closure and very old wound beads. Collection of the author.

Beadwork from Greenland

In Greenland, while men hunted whales, women made beaded shawl-type collars, which they developed around 1900 with the import of beads from Venice. Greenlanders had adorned themselves with beads for a long time using teeth, fish bones, bird claws and heads, pierced stones, and the few early glass beads brought by traders. At first the collars were small and the patterns simple. As beads became more available, the collars became larger and more elaborate. The deep collars are worn over warm clothing, adding lots of cheeriness but little warmth. The intricate geometric patterns with rhomboids (diamonds), zigzags, crosses, and other shapes are often passed from mother to daughter. The collars, which cover most of the upper body and extend from the shoulder to just above the elbow, have become a traditional costume and national symbol. When Danish Queen Margrethe II visited Greenland in 1997, she was presented with a traditional collar and an image of the Queen later appeared on a Greenland stamp. (Greenland is a protectorate of Denmark.)

This young Greenland woman wears the full traditional costume, which includes a beaded shawl-collar.
Bryan and Cherry Alexander Photography.

Beadwork for Royalty. This Greenland stamp shows Queen Margrethe II in traditional costume of West Greenland with an elaborate netted design. A white-tailed sea eagle soars in the background over Nuuk, the capital, with the famous landmark, the mountain Sermitsiaq, on the left. The stamp was designed and engraved by Martin Mörck from a photograph by Rigmor Mydstkov.

Ukrainian Beadwork

Netted beadwork traditions in the Ukraine go back at least a hundred years. A beadwork studio was established in the village of Vorontsovka in 1891 and beadwork soon spread through neighboring villages. For inspiration in their designs, Ukrainians turned to traditional patterns used in embroidery, weaving, and sewing, recreating crosses, circles, and other patterns. The Ukraine is located in the southeastern part of Central Europe near the Carpathian Mountains and the Black Sea.

Ukrainian beadwork, known as gerdany, has recently been documented and popularized by Canadian Maria Rypan in classes and books. Most popular are the broad netted collars of various widths, sometimes with a choker-type band, and flat bands of netted beadwork joined with a center medallion. Occasionally, bands of netted beadwork would be used to embellish pillbox-type hats. Girls and women of the mountains and foothill regions wore bands of netted beadwork stitched to red wool ribbons in their hair.

Using seed beads from neighboring (former) Czechoslovakia and nearby Venice, both prolific producers of seed beads for centuries, beaders created bright compositions of diamonds, crosses, drops, and, in some areas, stylized flowers and leaves. The colors used in each area were distinctive and indicated where the wearer lived. They range from the cool blue-whites of the northern provinces of Russia to the central region's soft, warm colors of rose and shades of gold, to the brighter primary colors used in the western Ukraine. In almost every village, some blue and violet were added.

Some information was taken from Maria Rypan's translation of *Charivni Vixzerunky by* E. M. Lytvynets, Kyyiv: Radianski Ukrainia, 1985.

An intricate netted band necklace with fringe made with size 18° to 22° beads. Possibly Russian or Ukrainian. Collection of the author.

Xhosa and Zulu Beadwork of South Africa

Xhosa women of South Africa often wear exquisite netted collars. While at first glance the collars may appear similar to other broad collars, they vary in at least one important way: the netting is more intricate because it is made of two layers, which are interlaced. These collars also have distinctive colors, usually opaque medium blue, dusty (Cheyenne) pink, white, and black. Some of the older netted collars were made with size 14° beads, making them very dense with little open space. Zulu women often wore bands of netting diagonally across their chest and also wore netted collars and belts.

A double weave netted Xhosa collar.
Collection of the author.

Xhosa woman wearing an intricate netted collar.
Photo collection of Carole Morris.

A Zulu belt with netted diamond pendants.
Collection of the author.

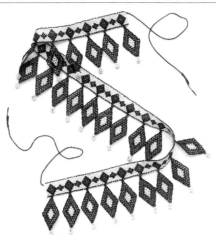

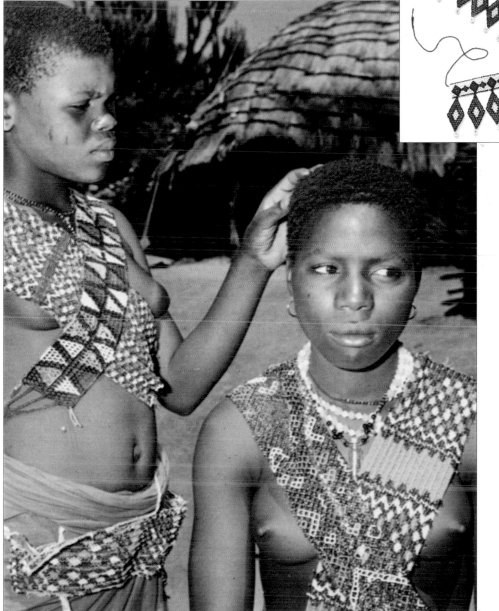

Zulu women wearing netted
beaded bands.
Photo collection of Carole Morris.

Sarawak Beadwork

Sarawak is the largest state in Malaysia and is located on the northwest coast of the island of Borneo. It is noted for its wide diversity of decorative arts, and beadwork is widely practiced. Sarawak beadwork is produced in many forms including hats, baskets, and adornments, but perhaps the best known object is the beaded baby carrier used by the Kelabits, Kenyahs, and Kayans. Known as a "ba," the carrier consists of a semicircular wooden seat with a curved back made of strips of plaited rattan. Rattan shoulder straps allow the mother to carry the seat on her back. The highly stylized design of netted beadwork is sewn to cloth and then to the back of the wooden seat. Its intricacy indicates the status of the child and his family. A child of an aristocratic family will have a very elaborate dragon-dog or human figure with hands and feet resembling curly tentacles. Children of more humble families will have less elaborate designs on their carriers such as a dog, deer, or other animal. Opaque beads in golden yellow (the dominant color), black, white, and green with touches of red brought by traders from Italy, Bohemia, and Japan are preferred. A typical baby carrier requires about sixteen thousand beads. The Kenyahs and Kayans also produce intricate netted patterns for hats and bowls.

Beadwork production is shared by men and women. Men compose and produce the design—earlier designs were carved on a board but more recently designs are drawn on paper. The drawing is pinned to a board and women work the pattern in netting over the drawing; these beaded designs often take weeks or months to complete. To begin, an anchor string is stretched across the top of the board and attached at each end. Next strings, often made of pineapple fiber or creepers, are at-

Little girl wearing a netted collar.
Photo collection of Carole Morris.

tached to the main cord with lark's head knots. Beads are added to the strings and some strings will go through two beads instead of one to connect them. Circular pieces begin from a ring in a similar fashion.

References

Beads: *Sarawak Museum Occasional Paper No. 2.* Kuching: Lee Ming Press, 1984.

Munan, Heidi. *Sarawak Crafts: Methods, Materials and Motifs.* Singapore: Oxford University Press, 1989, pp. 56–64.

Sheppard, Mubin. *Living Crafts of Malaysia.* Singapore: International Press, 1978, pp. 86–95.

Panel from a beaded Kelabit baby carrier. Collection of the author.

Large round netted beadwork is used as a hat cover. Collection of Carole Morris.

Beadwork of Egypt

Let us wrap up this short survey of netted beadwork with a look at a piece from the Museum of Fine Arts, Boston. The mummified body of Nes-mut-aat-neru, wife of Djedes-ief-ankh, a priest of ancient Egypt, was buried in a set of three coffins. She was a small, elderly woman who died about 700–675 B.C. After carefully preserving the body and wrapping it in a reddish shroud, a network of blue faience beads was laid over it, extending from the shoulders to the ankles. Attached to the netting near her heart are a winged scarab and figures of the Sons of Horus, all composed of beads. This type of netted beadwork was to become very popular in the following centuries, and hers is one of the earliest examples.

The mummy and netting were laid in an inner wooden coffin lined with plastered linen on which brightly colored decorations were painted. The outside of this coffin is beautifully decorated with a ram-headed falcon on the breast and intricate bands resembling a broad collar above. Below are panels separated by tri-colored bands that show uraeus serpents, an old-fashioned element, and scenes of the deceased adoring Osiris, a newer element, flanking them. Other deities with inscriptions fill the remaining panels. On the back, a painted column of inscriptions describes Nes-mut-aat-neru's ancestry.

This coffin was placed in a second coffin, which is much more simply decorated but exhibits fine artistry. The interior bottom of this coffin shows a figure of the "Goddess of the West" (a form of Hathor) in a graceful netted dress, which drapes diagonally across her hips. She is wearing a broad collar, earrings, bracelets, and anklets as well as a falcon headdress. The outside of the coffin shows a face, wig, and broad collar brightly painted on a layer of plaster with a winged sun disk, a small vignette and two columns of inscriptions below.

All of this was placed in an outer coffin, a rather austere rectangular wooden casket with four corner-posts and a domed lid on which sits a small black figure of a jackal, probably representing Anubis, at the foot end. The undecorated sides are of sycamore and an unidentified reddish wood. Inscriptions along the corner-posts honor Osiris and other gods. Edouard Naville, who discovered the tomb in 1894–95, found it buried deep in subterranean vaults beneath the mortuary temple of Queen Hatshepsut at Deir el-Bahri. Fortunately, this sanctuary had escaped detection by grave robbers.

Mummy of Nes-mut-aat-neru Egyptian, Late Period, Dynasty 25, about 700–675 B.C. Museum of Fine Arts, Boston. Gift of the Egypt Exploration Fund, 95.1407b © 2002 Museum of Fine Arts, Boston

LEFT: Mummy covered with a network of blue faience beads adorned with beaded figures of winged scarabs and figures of the Sons of Horus [Human remains/linen/faience Length: 151cm (59 7/16 in.)].

RIGHT: Inner coffin, which held the mummy [Plastered linen over wood Length: 169cm (66 7/16 in.)].
Excerpted from Mummies and Magic: The Funerary Arts of Ancient Egypt by Sue D'Auria, Peter Lacovara, and Catharine H. Roehrig; Boston: Northeastern University Press, 1988, pp. 173–175.

Netted Beadwork Basics

Let us begin with a definition of netted beadwork: a regular or irregular fabric of beads made with thread and one or more beads joined to a previous row either thread-to-bead or thread-to-thread and worked vertically, horizontally, diagonally, or randomly. While some would define all off-loom beadwork as netting if it is made by joining beads or threads without a supporting textile, for purposes of this book only netting that creates open spaces will be covered.

To limit the scope of the book, *Netted Beadwork* will *not* include:
- right-angle weave, triangle weave, or square stitch
- woven beadwork in which a fabric is created of warp and weft threads that go over and under and support the beads
- beadwork that is applied to a netted fabric or textile with sewing, embroidery, or tambour work
- braided beadwork in which strands of beads are interlaced.

Netted beadwork should not be confused with beaded netting, which refers to a netted fabric with beads sewn to it. It may also be referred to as mesh, web, webbing, lace, or lattice.

Netted beadwork is popular for several reasons: It requires fewer beads (and thus is lighter-weight) for the area that it covers than other types of beadwork, and it works up relatively quickly, drapes beautifully, and allows the underlying surface to be seen through the open spaces. Geometric patterns seem to be the most universal, but the stitch does not limit one to these shapes. With fine beads and a fine net, glorious flowers, leaves, birds, and many other shapes and designs can be portrayed. And, with a little practice, netting can be used to create or cover three-dimensional shapes.

Definition of Netting Terms

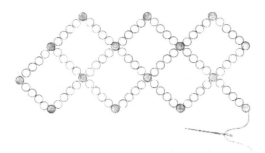

Beads that *join* two rows of beadwork will be referred to as **shared** beads because they are used in two rows and have two threads passing through them. In this illustration, they are the gray beads. Beads that connect the shared beads will be referred to as **bridge** beads and generally have one thread through them. They are the white beads. A sequence of bridge beads, shared bead(s), and bridge beads may be referred to as a **set** or *loop*.

Methods of Connecting Beads

Connecting Through Beads

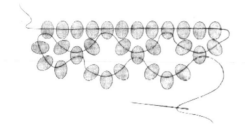

Perhaps the most common form of netted beadwork is three-bead netting in which the net is connected through the beads. Beginning with a multiple of four beads, the second row is added by stringing three beads and going back through every fourth bead of the first row. Subsequent rows are added by stringing three beads and going through the center bead of a three-bead set in the previous row. Five-bead, seven-bead, and larger netting would be worked in a similar manner.

Connecting by Looping Thread

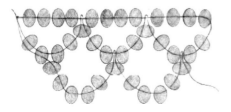

Netted beadwork can also be made by connecting between the beads, looping the working thread around the thread between the beads of the previous row and going back through the last bead added. There are various ways to end one row and begin the next—here the working thread is tied to the beginning thread.

Irregular or Random Netting

Random netting is made by adding loops of any size and connecting to any bead.

Edges for Flat Netting

There are many ways to work the edges of flat netting as shown on the left side of each illustration below. Netting may have one style of edge on one side and a different style on the other side.

Three-bead Netting with a Flat Edge

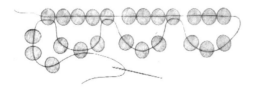

Three-bead Netting Around a Cord

(Attach to a string of beads or a clasp in a similar manner.)

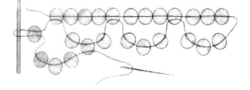

Three-bead Netting with a Picot Edge

(Picots may be one or more beads long.)

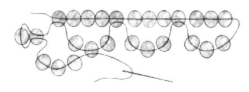

Three-bead Netting Attached to Other Beadwork

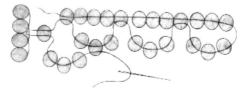

Three-bead Netting Attached to a Fabric Edge

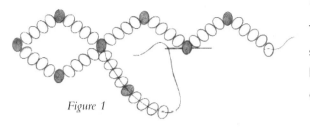

Figure 1

Tips

To ensure that your netting lays flat, pass the needle through shared beads so that it is parallel to the thread already in the hole. Do not angle your needle or cross or pierce the previous thread!

Bead netting will stretch or sag in the opposite direction from which it was worked. In other words, if the thread goes crosswise, the work may stretch lengthwise.

Increasing

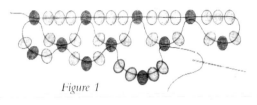

Figure 1

1. Increase by using more bridge beads in each set. (Area of increase shown with bold outline.)

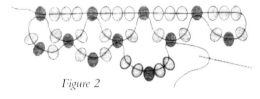

Figure 2

2. Increase by adding more shared beads.

Decreasing

Connect shared beads with fewer (or none) bridge beads than the previous row.

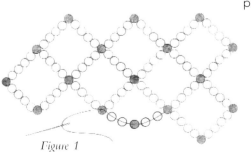

Figure 1

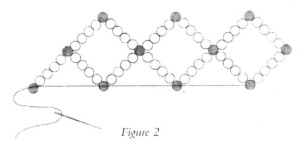

Figure 2

Tools and Techniques

Doing beadwork requires several small implements such as needles, scissors, ruler, thread, and other tools. If you keep all of these items in one convenient container, you won't be frustrated looking for a particular tool when you need it.

Tool Box

My tool box is a plastic pencil box about five by eight by two inches, which is large enough to hold a small project as well. When opened on my lap, the inside cover provides a workspace that can catch wayward beads. I've attached a magnetic plastic strip inside the cover with double-sided tape to temporarily hold needles. Following is a list of tools I keep in my kit.

Needles

I use a variety of needle sizes depending on the project. If picking up only one or two beads I may use a size 11 or 12 sharps needle. The size 12 is a finer needle and is about one and one-quarter inches long. If picking up several beads or scooping at random, I use a size 10 or 12 beading needle, which is two inches long. A thinner needle is needed if several passes must be made through the beads. I prefer the English needles made by the John James Company of Warwickshire, England. These carefully manufactured needles have smooth eyes that won't fray your thread.

Needle Containers

You may wish to have different containers for various needle sizes or types. These containers can be tube-shaped wooden needle holders beaded and personalized with your own design or you may wish to look for small tubular perfume bottles. The long, narrow cobalt blue bottle with a tasseled cap that held Evening in Paris perfume more than fifty years ago is ideal for two-inch beading needles. These bottles can often be found at flea markets or antique shows for $10–$20. A flat metal container about three by one-half by one-quarter inches that once held a small carpenter's pencil is also a possibility. You may also find small antique metal tube containers made to hold needles. The important thing is to find containers that work for you.

Scissors

One of your first investments should be a high-quality, small sharp scissors. Get the best you can afford, then guard against anyone using it for anything but cutting thread! A clean thread cut with a sharp scissors allows the thread to pass smoothly through the eye of the needle (a little spit helps, too). If you travel frequently, consider carrying the Thread Cutter Pendant, available at most bead stores, a nail clipper, or a dental floss container for clipping threads.

Thread

It seems that beaders prefer the type of thread that they started with because they've learned how to handle it. Both Silamide and Nymo are made of nylon and are strong and durable. However, neither are produced specifically for beadwork.

Silamide is made for hand tailoring and was originally put up in hanks of one-yard lengths, which, when doubled, were just right for hemming a sleeve cuff or pant leg. It is a twisted thread with a light wax coating and now is available in several colors. Size A, which is thin enough to pass through a bead several times, comes on large spools or cards of forty yards. Because it is a twisted thread, be sure to cut it cleanly and wax the end slightly before trying to put it through a needle eye.

Nymo is made for the leather industry for sewing shoes, purses, and belts. Because it is a non-twisted thread it is easier to thread in a needle than is Silamide. It comes in several weights: 00, 0, A, B, D, and F, which is the thickest. Generally, F is too thick to work well with size 11° seed beads or smaller. My all-around choice is size D, which works well with size 11° and 14° seed beads, and I usually carry about twenty bobbins of size D in different colors in my tool kit. Sizes 00 to B would be used for beads size 14° or smaller, depending on the project. Bobbins usually contain about eighty yards and spools about three hundred yards. You may notice the D weight on spools will feel slightly heavier than the D on bobbins. This is because the spools go on the top of a sewing machine and the bobbins go into the bobbin well. Spool thread is slightly thicker, slightly stronger, is bonded more tightly, and has a silicone coating to make it slip through the gears more easily. Bobbin thread flattens more easily and has a slight adhesive coating to keep it from unwinding.

Power Pro is a new thread on the market. It is highly resistant to abrasion and is able to withstand the sharp edges of crystals and certain glass beads, but this quality makes it somewhat more difficult to cut. The best way to cut it is to make a loop of thread and draw it along the blade of your scissors, pulling down as you draw it back and forth. The thread is advertised as a ``braided" thread, i.e. twisted, and waxed. Power Pro currently comes in only two colors, white and moss green, and is available in three sizes: .006, 10-lb. test; .009, 20-lb. test; and .011, 30-lb. test. The 10-lb. test will fit through a size 12 or 13 beading needle. Power Pro comes in twenty-eight- or one-hundred-yard spools and is the most expensive of these threads.

Monofilament fishing line can also be used for beadwork. I use it the least because over time it seems to become brittle and break. One manufacturer says that it has a five-year shelf life if it is not stored in direct sunlight. Much of this type of line is made to disintegrate out-of-doors so that it will not harm the environment. Its advantage is that it is clear and blends easily with all colors of beads.

Wax

Wax definitely has a place in my tool kit. At one time beeswax was probably used to protect cotton or silk thread or to stiffen the end of sinew or other fiber. I prefer microcrystalline wax, the composition beeswax that stays slightly soft for years and is now available at many bead stores. I use it to take the curliness out of the thread and to make two strands adhere to each other so they don't knot up. Wax can also be an aid to tighter tension and stiffer beadwork. Thread Heaven, a silicone conditioner, is great for bead embroidery and keeping thread from tangling.

Lighter

Many beaders use a cigarette lighter to slightly melt the tiny bit of thread that extends beyond a knot at the end of their thread. This prevents the little fuzzy thread ends from protruding from a bead and making your work look unprofessional. If you're uneasy about using a cigarette lighter or have trouble gripping one, consider using a grill lighter which is ignited with a pistol-type grip. (See Adding New Thread below for more details.)

Nail Polish

I use a dab of clear nail polish to prevent knots from coming undone. Some beaders like to use watch crystal cement, which has a very fine tip for applying the glue, but I find it too cumbersome and time consuming to put the tiny stopper back in the tube. Also, nail polish is cheaper. But be sure it is fresh. The solvent in the nail polish slightly melts the nylon causing it to adhere to itself. If you must remove a knot coated with nail polish, soften it first with nail polish remover.

Ruler or Tape Measure

I carry both a roll-up tape measure and a six-inch ruler.

Knot Remover

A curved tweezers with a pointed tip is an indispensable tool. To remove a knot, hold the knot over your fingertip, squeeze the tweezers points together, then plunge them into the heart of the knot and let them open. Repeat the process until the knot loosens. I can't guarantee that all knots are removable with this technique but I've had very good success.

Hemostat

A hemostat is a surgical tool that looks something like a scissors, but instead of blades, it has points like a tweezers that can lock together by squeezing the handles. This tool is handy for grabbing the needle when it is in an awkward position. A piece of a wide rubber band also works well.

Techniques

Adding New Thread

This method of adding thread is quick, easy and secure, so don't use thread longer than you can pull in one stroke, usually about one and one-half to two yards of thread. When you have four to five inches of thread left, it's time to tie on a new length. Leave the needle on the thread in the beadwork. Thread a new needle and knot the end. Clip the tail close to the knot and melt it slightly with a lighter. Bring the needle through four to six beads of the existing work and bring the thread out of the same bead and in the same direction as the old thread. Tie the old thread to the new thread with a square knot. Pull tightly so the knot is buried in the bead hole if possible. Bring the old thread (with the needle still on it) through four to six beads and clip it off close to the beads. Dab the knot with clear nail polish. You're all set to keep beading!

Square Knot

Left thread goes over the right thread and around it. Then the right thread goes over the left thread and passes through the loop.

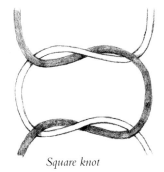

Square knot

Knotting Between Beads

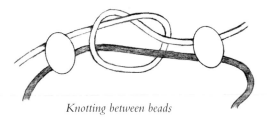

Knotting between beads

Pass the working thread (light color in illustration) under the thread between the bead your thread just exited and the next bead, then pass the thread through the loop just formed. Pull tight to secure the knot. Pass the working thread through the next bead.

Overhand Knot

Use this knot at the end of a new thread on your needle.

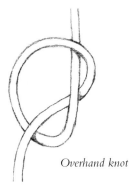

Overhand knot

Lark's Head Knot

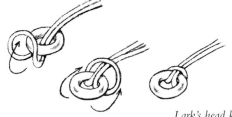

Lark's head knot

projects

· · · · · ·

Lace Chain

This basic chain can be used as a necklace, as a support for a pouch, or it can be manipulated in several ways. Gather and roll it to make a flower, cover a large bead with it or use it as a connecting element between two other pieces of beadwork. The chain is worked back and forth in a zigzag fashion. It is a pattern that has been used for close to a hundred years!

Supplies

Size 11° or other size seed beads
Nylon thread (preferably Nymo D)

1. Tie 1 bead on the end of your thread, leaving a 6" tail. This bead will be part of your work.

Figure 1

2. Add 5 more beads and go back through the second last bead, counting from the needle end of the thread (picot made).

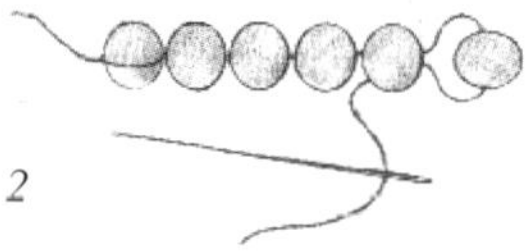

Figure 2

3. Add 3 beads and go into the first bead on the thread (the one tied on).

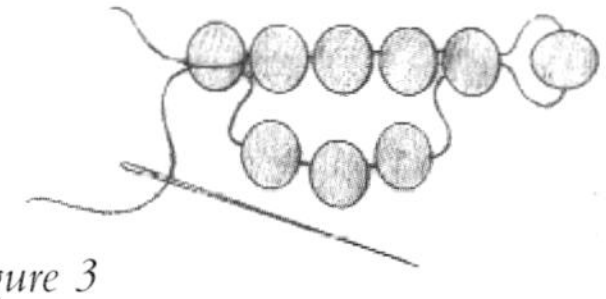

Figure 3

4. Add 3 beads and go back through the second last bead (as in Step 2, picot made).

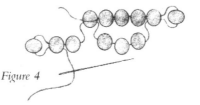

Figure 4

5. Add 3 beads and go into the middle bead of the last set of 3 beads.

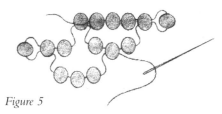

Figure 5

6. Add 3 beads and go back through the second last bead.

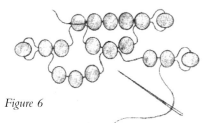

Figure 6

7. Add 3 beads and go into the middle bead of the last set of 3 beads.

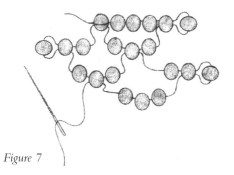

Figure 7

8. Repeat Steps 4 through 7 until the chain is desired length.

Hint: To help your work go faster, hold the working edge of the chain parallel to your left forefinger. To change directions, move your hand but do not turn the work over. To tighten the picots, slide the 3 beads against the work. Wrap the thread over your forefinger and hold in place with your middle finger. Put your needle into the second last bead, then hold the beads in place with your thumb while you draw the thread tight.

Variations

1. Make Wider Chains

Increase the number of beads in the picot. Instead of adding 3 beads, you might add 4. Then go back through 2 instead of 1.

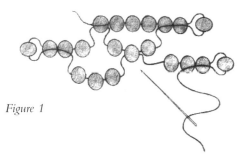

Figure 1

4. Make Color Patterns

Patterns may be made to form zigzags, diamonds or triangles within the chain.

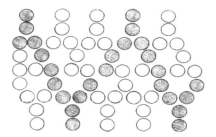

2. Increase the number of sets in Steps 1 and 2. For example, begin with 10 beads instead of 6 and make 2 loops instead of 1. The chain may be made in almost any width—the number of beads must be divisible by 4, then add 2.

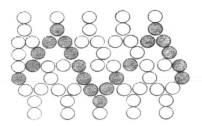

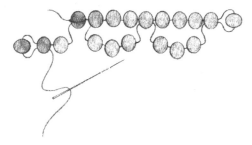

Figure 2

3. Vary Bead Type

Replace the center bead in a set with a 3 mm crystal or use a crystal instead of the second last bead in the picot.

• • • • • •

Easy Netted Bead

These beads are quick to make and can be embellished once completed. To make one, you'll make a strip of netting with picots on both sides long enough to go around the equator of the bead, then join the ends, gather the bottom edge, slip in a wooden bead, gather the top edge and presto! You have a beaded bead! After you've made one, try it with different beads or make patterns using different colors.

Supplies

Plastic or wooden bead, 14 mm
Size 11° seed beads, 4 grams
Nylon thread (preferably Nymo D)

1. Thread your favorite needle with a single strand of thread about 1½ yd long; tie 1 bead on the end of the thread leaving a 3" tail. This bead will be left in your work.

Figure 1

2. Add 10 more beads. Go back through the second and third last beads (picot made).

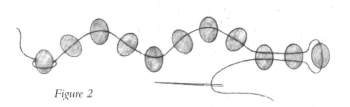

Figure 2

3. Add 3 beads. Go into the fourth bead in the previous row counting from where your thread exited a bead (3-bead loop made). Repeat this step once. Your thread should now be exiting the tied-on bead.

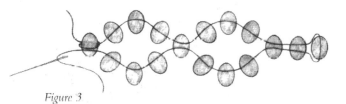

Figure 3

4. Add 4 beads. Go back through the second and third last beads (picot made).

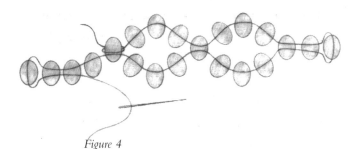

Figure 4

5. Add 3 beads. Go into the middle bead of the next 3-bead loop in the previous row. Repeat this step once. Add 4 beads and go back through the second and third last beads.

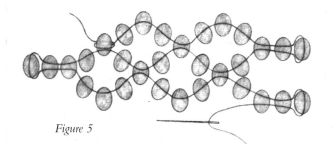

Figure 5

6. Repeat Steps 3, 4, and 5 until there are 11 picots on one side and 10 on the other side and you have just come out of a picot. You will now be on the side opposite the tied-on bead.

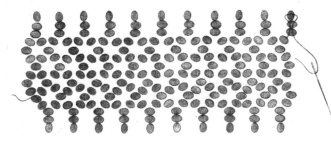

Figure 6

7. Lace up the sides to form a tube. Hold the ending edge and the beginning edge so they are almost next to each other. Add 1 bead. Go into the middle bead of the loop on the opposite side. Repeat 3 more times. (The new beads are shown with a bold outline.)

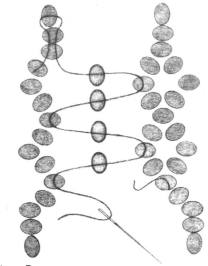

Figure 7

8. Add 4 beads. Go back through the second and third last beads. Add 1 bead. Go into the tied-on bead (Figure 8). Knot thread between the beads (see page 27).

9. Pass thread through beads to opposite side so that thread is exiting a bead on the tip of the picot. Pass the thread through all the tip beads on that side. Pull thread tight so that the tip beads are touching and the piece forms a cup. Go through all tip beads again. Knot thread between the beads.

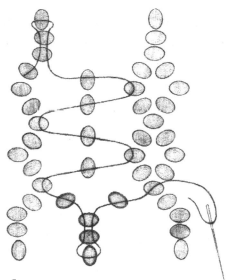

Figure 8

10. Pass thread to other side of work and go through all tip beads. Place 14-mm bead in the cup just formed with the hole facing the hole in the bottom of the cup. Pull thread tight to close the cup. Go through all tip beads again. To keep the 14-mm bead in place, pass the needle through it. Catch a tip bead from the other side and go back to the first side. Do this once more. Knot the thread and weave in the tails.

Adjustments

If your seed beads are large size 11°, you may need to reduce the number of beads in the picot from 2 to 1 on one or both sides. You may also need to make only 10 picots on one side and 9 on the other. For a smaller or larger base bead, you may need to increase or decrease the number of beads in the picot and the number of picots on each side.

- Use size 14° seed beads with a 10-mm base bead. Reduce the number of picots in Step 6 to 10 on one side and 9 on the other.

- Use Delicas with a 12-mm base bead.

Jane Langenback

Variations

- Add ruffles. (See instructions for Ruffle Bracelet on page 53.)

- Replace the middle bead of each 3-bead loop with a 3-mm crystal.

- Sew beads in the spaces formed by the netting.

Color in your own pattern.

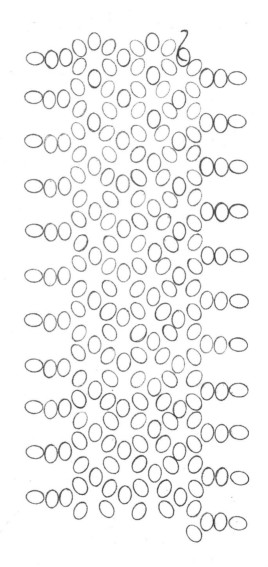

Rose Hamerlinck

• • • • • •

Netted Bezel for a Cabochon

A bezel for a cabochon can be made using the instructions for the Easy Netted Bead. To measure the length needed to go around the cabochon, take a narrow strip of paper and place it around the cab. Fold the paper back to indicate where the edges meet. Size 14° beads are recommended.

Supplies

Flat-back cabochon
Size 14° seed beads
Nylon thread (preferably Nymo D)

Make a strip of netting as long as your paper strip and join the edges as you would for an Easy Netted Bead. Knot the thread and pass your needle through beads so it is exiting a tip bead. Add 1 bead between each tip bead for the underside of the cabochon. (Adjust as necessary depending on the size and shape of your cabochon.) Pull thread so the edge gathers. Knot thread and pass needle through to a tip bead on the front side. Add 2 beads between each tip bead. Place cabochon in the bezel and pull the top edge tight and knot. Go through all tip beads on both the front and underside again.

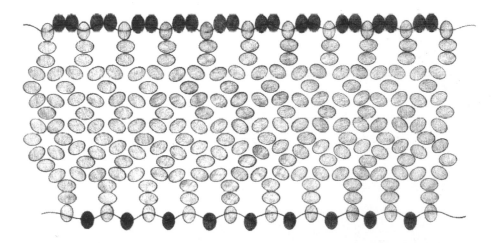

• • • • • •

Flowers and Leaves

Once you've mastered the Lace Chain, you can make flowers using this chain by gathering one edge, rolling the gathered strip and sewing it as you roll it. Leaves are easy as well. You'll begin them with a center spine, then do netting on either side with decreases along the beginning and ending edges.

Pom-pom Flowers

Supplies

Size 11° or 14° seed beads, 3 grams
Nylon thread (preferably Nymo D)

Following the instructions on page 31, make a strip of Lace Chain with thirty-six picots on each side. Knot thread between the beads (see page 27). Pass the needle through to the tip bead on the opposite side of the last picot made. Now go through all the tip beads on this side. At the end of the strip, pull the thread so the beads are gathered together and touching. Knot thread between the beads to hold the gather in place. This will be the bottom of the pom-pom.

Form a ring with the last 5 tip beads by going forward through them again (these are the 32nd through 36th tip beads). Begin rolling the gathered edge around the 5-bead ring, stitching the tip beads from the gathered edge of the strip to the 5-bead ring as shown. For every single bead on the ring, go through 2 beads on the gathered edge of the strip (see Figures 1 and 2).

When you've made 1 complete roll, stitch the tip beads from the gathered edge of the strip to the second ring formed. Continue rolling and stitching until you reach the end of the strip.

Figure 1

Figure 2

Variations

- Replace the 2 beads below the tip bead in the picot on one side with a 3-mm crystal or 3- or 4-mm bi-cone crystal (see Crystal Collar on page 103 for illustration).

- Use a shiny silver-lined bead for the tip of the picot on one side.

Rose on Netted Base

Supplies

Size 11° or 14° seed beads
Nylon thread (Preferably Nymo D)

Netted Base

Row 1: String 5 beads and tie into a loop with a square knot, leaving a 3"–4" tail and keeping the tension tight.

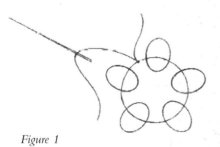

Figure 1

Row 2: Add 1 bead and go into the next bead. Do this 4 more times. You will have a 5-pointed star. Go through the first bead of Row 2 (the row you just finished) so your thread is coming out of a point of the star.

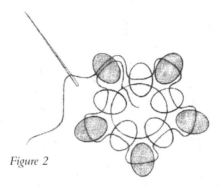

Figure 2

Row 3: Add 3 beads and go into the next star point bead. Do this 4 more times.

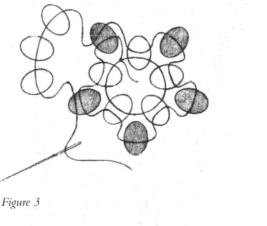

Figure 3

At the end of the row go through the first 2 beads of Row 3, the one just finished, bringing you to the point of the newly formed, larger star (Figure 4). Push the beads into place so that they form a star.

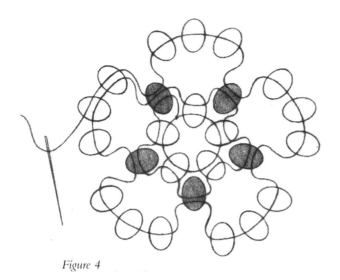

Figure 4

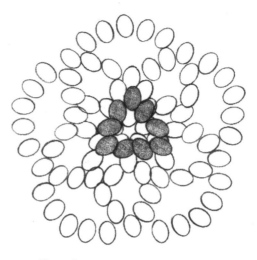

Figure 5

Row 4: Add 5 beads and go into the next star point. Do this 4 more times (Figure 5).

Form the Petals

Bring the thread to the center of the flower base by going through beads. Sew 1 to 3 yellow beads across the center, then add 3-bead loops as follows: With your thread exiting one of the beads in the beginning 5-bead ring, pick up 3 beads. Skip the next bead in the 5-bead ring and go into the second bead. Continue to pick up 3 beads and go into a bead 1 bead away, following a path that spirals outward from the center of the rose. As you reach the outer ring of beads, you may want to pick up 5 beads instead of 3 and go into the third or fourth bead away.

Variations

• Make petals with 10 beads instead of 3.

• Add crystals to the petal tips.

• Make petals as shown in Figure 6 between every pair of beads.

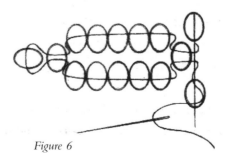

Figure 6

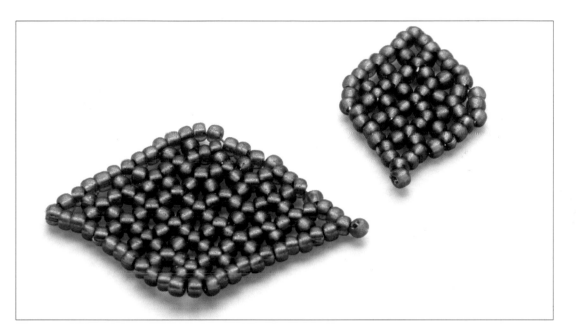

Netted Leaf

Supplies

Size 11° or 14° seed beads
Nylon thread (Preferably Nymo D)

1. With 1 yd of thread (threaded singly) in your needle, tie 1 bead in the middle of the thread. (This bead will remain in your work.) String on 17 more beads (or for a larger leaf, add a multiple of 4 plus 1 after the tied-on bead). Go back through the second last bead counting from the needle end of the thread.

2. Add 3 beads. Go forward into the fourth bead counting from where your thread exited a bead.

3. Repeat from Step 2 three more times so that your thread is coming out of the tied-on bead (Figure 1).

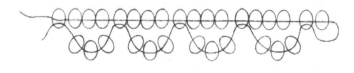

Figure 1

4. Without adding any beads, turn and go back through the last 2 beads of the last set of 3 beads, so that you are coming out of a shared bead (Figure 2).

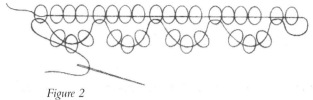

Figure 2

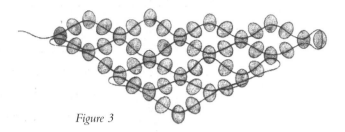

Figure 3

5. Add 3 beads. Go forward into the middle bead of the next set of 3 beads. Repeat this step 2 more times.

6. Continue going back and forth until there is only 1 set of 3 in the row. Go through the center bead of the next set in the previous row, knot thread, and weave in tail (Figure 3).

7. Work the other side of the leaf in the same manner using the thread tail. To begin, pass your needle to the middle bead of the set of 3 beads.

Knotted Netted Necklace or Bracelet

This necklace or bracelet is constructed of netting attached at each end to a seven-strand clasp. After the netting is completed, a simple overhand knot is tied in the middle of the netting. Arrange the knot so that it forms a pleasing "V" in the center of the piece. About three and one-half to four inches will be taken up for the knot and shrinkage (the difference between the length of the initial strand and the strands after they are worked). Allow slightly less for a narrower piece. You may also make the necklace in a longer length. To make a bracelet, begin by measuring your wrist, then calculate the length by substituting your wrist measurement in the formula below.

Calculate	length for a necklace	for a bracelet
Finished length	18"	7¼"
Subtract for clasp	-1"	-1"
Add for knot	+ 3½"	+ 3½"
Length of first strand	20½"	9¾"

Supplies

7-Strand Clasp*

Size 11° seed beads: 30 grams for necklace, 15 grams for bracelet

Size 8° triangle beads**: 30 grams for necklace, 15 grams for bracelet

Nylon thread (preferably Nymo D)

*A 3-strand clasp may be substituted by connecting 2 or 3 rows of netting to each hole of the clasp.

**Size 8 seed beads may be substituted for triangle beads.

Thread a 4-yd piece of thread in a beading needle. Bring ends together and knot. Clip ends close to the knot and with a lighter melt the knot slightly. Wax thread so the 2 strands adhere to each other.

Attaching Thread to Clasp

Pass the needle through the outside hole of the first side of the clasp, pulling the thread so that the knot is almost at the clasp. Separate the 2 strands between the clasp and the knot. Pass the needle between the strands. Pull tight so that the knot is near the clasp (Figure 1).

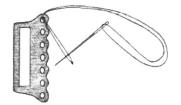

Figure 1

Row 1: Pick up sets of 7 seed beads and 1 triangle bead to equal the length needed for your necklace or bracelet. If the multiple of 7 + 1 doesn't add up to the desired length, add extra sets. Be sure there are an odd number of sets. Then add 7 more seed beads. Pass the needle through the first hole of the right side of the clasp. Go back through the last seed bead added (Figure 2).

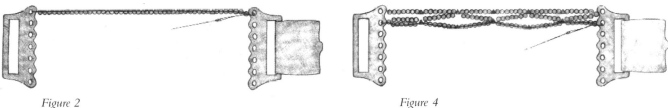

Figure 2

Row 2: Pick up 6 seed beads, 1 triangle bead, and 7 seed beads. Pass your needle through the second triangle bead of the previous row. Continue to pick up 7 seed beads, 1 triangle bead and 7 seed beads and pass your needle through the second triangle bead along the previous row until you reach the left side of the clasp. Pass your needle through the second hole of the clasp, then back through the last bead added (Figure 3).

Figure 3

Row 3: Pick up 6 seed beads. Pass your needle through the first triangle bead of the previous row. Continue to pick up 7 seed beads, 1 triangle bead, and 7 seed beads and pass your needle through the second triangle bead along the previous row until you reach the right side of the clasp. Pass your needle through the next hole of the clasp, then back through the last bead added (Figure 4).

Figure 4

Continue working back and forth between the 2 sides of the clasp until there are 13 rows. After coming out of the clasp, go back through a few beads and knot between the beads (see page 27). Go through a few more beads and knot again. Go through a few more beads and clip remaining thread close to the work. Apply clear nail polish to the knots.

Tie an overhand knot in the center of the completed beadwork. If the bracelet is too large, untie the knot and add one more row of netting to the last hole of the clasp (there will then be two rows attached to this hole.)

Netted Cuff

This simple netted cuff is worked along the length of the bracelet. It can be worn as is or embellished with ruffles (see Ruffle Bracelet on page 53) or loops. Pom-pom or Rose Flowers and Leaves (see pages 41–46) may be added to make a wrist corsage.

Supplies

Size 10° or 11° seed beads

Nylon thread (preferably Nymo D) in a color to match your beads

One large or two medium snaps, depending on width of bracelet

Creating the Base

Measure your wrist and add 1¼". Thread a needle with a single strand of thread about 1½ yd long. Leaving a 6" tail, string on 1 bead and go through it again to serve as a stopper bead, which will be removed later.

Row 1: String on a multiple of 4 beads until you have a strand the circumference of your wrist plus 1¼". Add 3 beads. Go back through the seventh bead on the string, counting from the needle end.

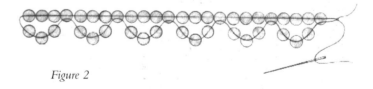

Figure 1

Row 2: String on 3 beads. Skip 3 beads and go into the fourth bead, making a loop. Continue to the end of the strand (Figure 1). Slip off the stopper bead and tie the thread to the tail. Leave the tail hanging—you can use it later to sew on a snap or button closure (Figure 2).

Figure 2

Row 3: Add 3 beads and go back through the center bead of the loop just finished. Continue adding 3-bead loops and going into the center bead of the next loop in the previous row until you reach the end of the row. At the end, add 3 beads and go back in the opposite direction (Figure 3).

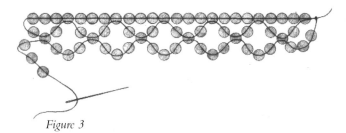

Figure 3

Work back and forth until your bracelet is the desired width, ending at the opposite end from the beginning. Knot thread between 2 beads (see page 27) and use this thread to sew a snap to this end of the bracelet. Sew the other half of the snap to the other end so the ends overlap about ½".

Ruffle Bracelet

Supplies

Size 11° seed beads, about 30 grams total in 1 or more
  colors
Nylon thread (Preferably Nymo D)

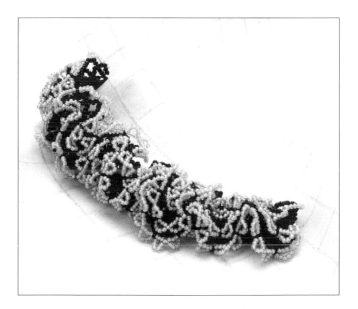

The Ruffle Bracelet was one of my earliest classes when I began teaching in the late 1980s. A group of beaders invited me to Northfield, Minnesota, to teach a class in netting. Although I really didn't know much about netting at the time, I agreed and got busy creating a class for them. The Ruffle Bracelet was the result and it has always been one of my favorites. It is created in two parts: a flat netted base and ruffles of beads made from increasing netting, which stand up from the base.

A ruffle of beads can be added to a string of seed beads, a beaded edge or a base of beads created with netting. The ruffle stitch is also called the "Ogalalla Butterfly" stitch by Horace Goodhue in his book *Indian Bead-Weaving Patterns*. It is made with increasing netting with each row having more beads added in each set, i.e. sets of 3 in the first row, sets of 5 in the second row, sets of 7 in the third row, and so on.

Complete a Netted Cuff (see page 51) but do not add the snap yet. This will be used as the base.

Thread a needle with a single thread, 1½ yd long. Knot the end and melt the knot. Bring the needle through a few beads so that it exits the first shared bead of the middle row at one end of the bracelet. Anchor thread with a second knot between the beads (see page 27). The first row will be worked lengthwise in the middle row of the cuff.

Row 1: Pick up 3 beads. Pass the thread through the next shared bead of the middle row—you will be working lengthwise toward the opposite end of the bracelet

(Figure 1). Continue doing this the length of your bracelet, stopping ½" from the end of the row, leaving space for the snap closure, which will be added later. Turn your work, add 3 beads, and pass the needle through the middle bead of the last loop of beads just formed (Figure 2).

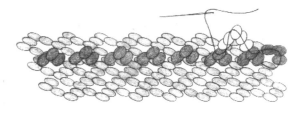

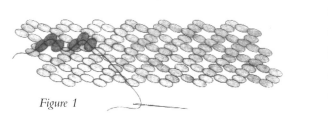

Figure 1

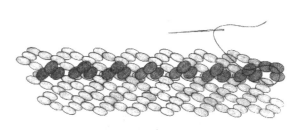

Figure 2

Row 2: Pick up 5 beads and go through the middle bead (this will be your shared bead) of each loop formed in Row 1 (the 3-bead loops). Continue picking up 5 beads and going through the middle bead of each loop in the previous row (Figure 3). At the end of the row, add 5 beads, turn your work and pass the needle through the middle bead of the last loop of beads just formed.

Figure 3

Row 3: Pick up 7 beads and go through the middle bead of each loop formed in Row 2 (the 5-bead loops). Continue picking up 7 beads and going through the middle bead of each loop in the previous row. At the end of the row, add 5 beads, turn your work and pass the needle through the middle of the last loop of beads just formed.

Row 4: Pick up 9 beads and go through the middle bead of each loop formed in Step 3 (the 7-bead loops). Continue picking up 9 beads and going through the middle bead of each loop in the previous row. At the end of the row, add 7 beads, turn your work and pass the needle through the middle of the last loop of beads just formed.

Variation for Row 4 (Double Loops): Pick up 5 beads and go through the middle bead of the next loop. Pick up 5 more beads and go through the middle bead of the loop from the row below.

Complete Rows 1–4 once or twice more on each side of the center row. If you wish, repeat rows 1– 4 on each lengthwise edge of the bracelet as well. Substitute size 6° or 8° seed beads or stone chips for 1 or 2 beads in the last row of each ruffle.

Random Netting

Elizabeth Ofstead

Random netting is quick and easy to make. I make several flat pancake-size pieces, then assemble them into a larger fabric. The netting may be as open or as dense as you like. You can control this by the number of beads you scoop onto your needle.

Supplies

Size 11° seed beads (size 14°, other sizes, or a mix may also be used)
Nylon thread (preferably Nymo D)

To begin, thread a beading needle with 2 yd of thread, bring the ends together and knot. Clip the tail close to the knot and melt the knot using a lighter. Wax thread so the strands stick together and don't tangle. Scoop* a needleful of beads (about ¾ 1") and go through the first several beads again to close the loop. Scoop another needleful of beads and go through any bead or beads in the first loop. Scoop again and go through another bead. Keep your work flat by holding the piece between your thumb and forefinger. (Figures 1–3).

*Scooping

Place an ounce or so of beads in a box that is about 4 × 4 × ½" deep. Mound them up in one corner. Holding the needle between your thumb and middle finger, pass the needle through the middle of the mound of beads with a slight upward motion. Avoid pushing the needle along the bottom where there is less likelihood of catching beads.

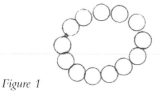

Figure 1

Figure 2

Figure 3

Making a Pocket to Encase an Object

To encase a flat object such as a button, cabochon, coin, shell, flattened bottle cap, or other object, make a background piece of random netting the desired size. Then make another piece slightly larger than the object to be encased. Weave the 2 pieces together with the smaller piece to the back to make a pocket. Slip the object into the pocket and continue weaving to close the pocket. Join several small pockets to form a necklace, or use one to make a pin.

Other Effects

Random netting may be used as a fill-in or connecting net between other parts or as a base to which other parts are attached. To make a large piece of random netting, make several small pieces about 3"–4" in diameter, then join them with short bead strands (Figure 4).

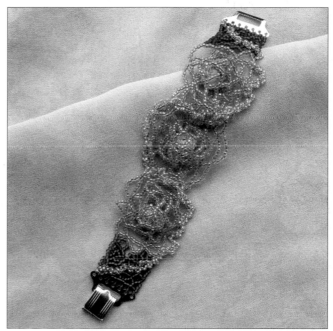

Doris Coghill

For a 3-dimensional effect, work more netting over the top of your piece, creating a mossy or tangled vine effect. Make a frilly edge by increasing the number of loops or the number of beads in each loop as you work around the outside of the piece.

Figure 4

• • • • • •

Victorian Netted Tulip Pouch

The inspiration for this pouch came from a beaded bag I saw in a museum. We will work netting vertically, meaning that beads are added working up and down rather than across, back and forth, or around. After we have worked around the top ring with vertical rows, the rows will be joined so that the bag is closed, like a seam. Then we bring the bottom together by connecting the bottom beads with decreasing rows of peyote stitch. Finally, a tassel, necklace strap, and fringe are added.

Supplies

Size 10° or 11° seed beads: 30 grams of the main color and 10 grams of the accent color

One large bead (up to ¾" diameter) for the tassel

30–40 small beads (approximately 3–5 mm) for necklace strap, fringes, and tassel

Nylon thread (preferably Nymo D)

Small piece (approximately 6" × 6") of silk or other fabric for lining

1. Thread your needle with a single thread, 1½ yd long. String on 80 beads and tie the thread with a square knot so the beads form a ring (Figure 1). This will be the top of the bag. If you wish, every fifth bead (these will be the shared beads) may be a contrasting color.

2. Continuing with the same thread that is attached to the ring of beads, string on 13 sets of the following: 5 bridge beads and 1 shared bead. (For a shorter bag use 11 sets, for a longer bag, use 15 sets.) Do not add a shared bead in the last set.

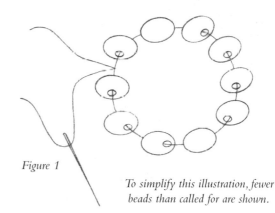

Figure 1

To simplify this illustration, fewer beads than called for are shown.

3. Go back through (toward the top of the bag) the fourth shared bead counting from the needle end of the thread (Figure 2).

4. String on 5 bridge beads, 1 shared bead, and 5 bridge beads. Continuing toward the top of the bag, go through the second shared bead from the one you just went through.

5. After going through the last shared bead near the top of the bag, add 5 bridge beads and go through the next shared bead to the *right* in the top ring (Figure 3).

6. Add 5 bridge beads, 1 shared bead, and 5 bridge beads and go through the second shared bead working your way towards the bottom of the bag. At the end of the row add 5 bridge beads, 1 shared bead, 5 bridge beads, 1 shared bead, and 5 bridge beads. Turn and go through the fourth shared bead up the chain (Figure 4).

7. Continue working up and down until you are at the bottom of the bag and there are no more shared beads left in the top ring. This row will connect the 2 edges of the bag. Pick up 5 bridge beads, 1 shared bead and 5 bridge beads and go through the shared bead on the opposite edge. Then add 5 bridge beads and go through the shared bead on the opposite side (Figure 5). Continue to the top of the bag as though you are lacing the sides together.

Knot thread between two beads (see page 27) and weave in the tail. Coat the knot with clear nail polish.

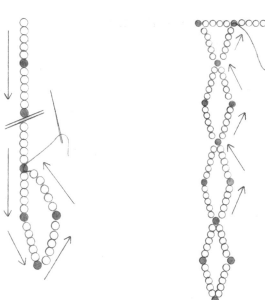

Figure 2   Figure 3

Figure 4   Figure 5

Close the Bottom of the Bag

Close the bottom of the bag by connecting the shared beads as follows. Anchor a new thread and bring it through a shared bead on the bottom of the bag. Add a bead and go through the next shared bead around the bottom. Continue adding 1 bead between each shared bead until all the bottom shared beads are connected (Figure 6). Go through the first shared bead again. Draw thread up tight and knot between beads but do not cut your thread.

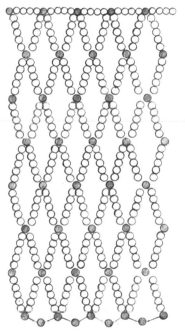

Figure 6

You will fill in the bottom of the bag with even-count peyote stitch, which means that at the end of each row you must "step up to the next row," or to be specific, go through the last bead of the previous row and the first bead of the row you just finished.

Row 1: Do 1 row of peyote stitch (16 beads "sticking up") as follows: Add 1 bead and go into the second bead counting from where your thread exited a bead (Figure 7).

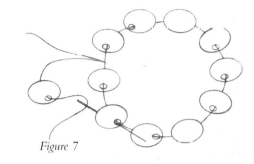

Figure 7

Each bead added is "1 peyote stitch." At the end of the row, "step up" to do the next row. To "step up," complete the row, then go through the first bead added for this row (Figure 8).

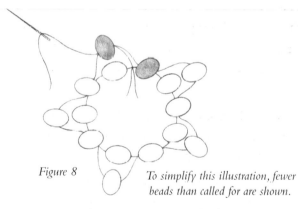

Figure 8   *To simplify this illustration, fewer beads than called for are shown.*

Row 2: Peyote 3, skip 1 (decrease made, figure 9). Repeat 3 more times (12 beads sticking up).

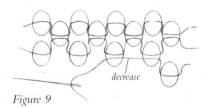

decrease

Figure 9

Row 3: Work 1 row of peyote stitch.

Row 4: Peyote 2, skip 1. Repeat 3 more times (8 beads sticking up).

Row 5: Work 1 row of peyote stitch.

Row 6: Peyote 1, skip 1. Repeat 3 more times (4 beads sticking up).

Row 7: Work 1 row of peyote stitch. Go through first bead of last row and all sticking up beads. Knot between the beads (see page 27).

Adding the Tassel

Using the same thread used to finish the bottom of the bag, go through the large bead, add a strand of beads, then go back up through the strand (skipping the very bottom bead) and the large bead. Go through a bead in the bottom of the bag and back down again through the large bead. Continue until you have the desired number of strands to form a tassel, going through the large bead each time (Figure 10).

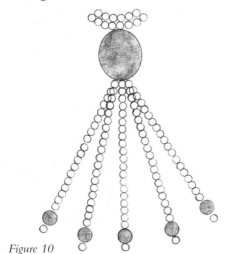

Figure 10

Attaching the Necklace Strap

Thread a needle with 2 yd of thread and bring the ends together to form a double strand. Anchor the thread in the beginning ring of beads. String on 24" of beads using seed beads and other beads in the pattern of your choice. Connect strand to opposite side of pouch with a knot between the beads (see page 27). Weave in tail.

Adding Fringe

Knot a single strand of thread and melt the knot. Bring the thread through 4 beads from top to bottom so that it comes out of a shared bead in the first row of shared

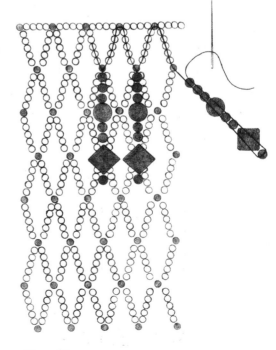

Figure 11

beads below the top edge. Knot between the beads (see page 27). Add a strand of fringe (as shown in Figure 11 or your own version) and go back through the strand skipping the bottom bead, which holds the beads on the strand. Bring your thread through the 5 beads above and to the right of the shared bead. Now go down through the 5 five beads to the right, again coming out of a shared bead in the first row of shared beads below the top edge. Add another strand of fringe. Continue around the bag, ending by knotting between beads twice and burying the ends. Seal knots with clear nail polish and clip excess thread. (Note there are 16 strands of fringe.)

Lining the Pouch

Measure the distance around the inside of the top of your bag and the length of the bag. Add 1" to each measurement. Cut a piece of fabric this size. Fold fabric in half lengthwise and sew a ½" seam. Hem the seam edge. On the bottom edge, fold up ½" toward the inside and sew with a running stitch. Pull the thread tight to gather the fabric, forming the bottom of the pouch. Knot thread. Hem the top edge. Insert lining into pouch and stitch to the top row of beads.

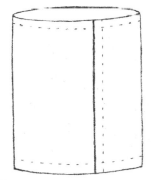

Figure 12

Ornaments

With some adjustments to the Victorian Tulip Pouch, this basic pattern can be used for a Netted Easter Egg, a Christmas Ornament or a Soap Dispenser Cover.

Netted Easter Egg

Supplies

Styrofoam egg, 2½" tall

Colored foil to cover the egg

Size 11° seed beads; 20 grams for bridge beads (BB), 10 grams for shared beads (SB)

Small beads for embellishment (optional)

Nylon thread (preferably Nymo D)

Work as for Victorian Tulip Pouch (see page 59). For the beginning ring, which will sit on top of the narrow end of the egg, string on 30 beads with every second bead being a shared bead color. String on 11 sets of the following: 5 bridge beads and 1 shared bead. Skip the shared bead in the last set. Go back through (toward the top of the netting) the fourth shared bead counting from the needle end. Continue in pattern around the beginning ring. To form the netting into a tube, follow instructions for the Victorian Tulip Pouch, Step 7.

Finishing

Slip the Styrofoam egg into the net and close bottom with peyote stitch as follows:

Row 1: Add 3 beads in the bridge bead color (BB) between each shared bead. Go through the first 3 BB again. Draw thread up tight and knot between beads.

Row 2: Add 1 bead in the shared bead (SB) color between each set of 3 beads. Go through the first SB again.

Row 3: Add 2 BB between each SB. Go through the first 2 BB again.

Row 4: Repeat Row 2.

Row 5: Repeat Row 3.

Row 6: Repeat Row 2.

Row 7: Add 1 BB between each SB. Go through the first BB again.

Row 8: Repeat Row 2.

Row 9: Repeat Row 7.

Row 10: Repeat Row 2. Knot between the beads and weave in the tail. Dab clear nail polish on the knot. Clip end.

Netted Christmas Ornament

Supplies

Plain Christmas ornament, 2½" round

Size 11° seed beads: 25 grams for bridge beads (BB),
*   10 grams for shared beads (SB)*

Nylon thread (preferably Nymo D)

You can use the directions for the Easter Egg to embellish a 2½" round Christmas ornament by making a few simple changes. Make the netting off the

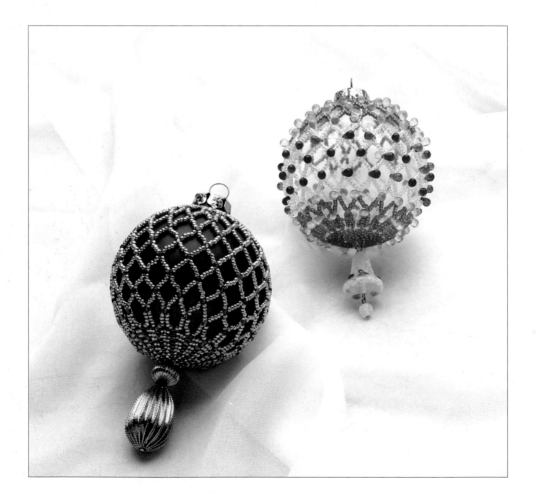

ornament, then place it on the ball and connect the bottom point beads following the instructions above for closing the bottom of the Easter Egg.

Make the initial ring by stringing on 18 sets of 3 beads for a total of 54 beads; every third bead is a shared bead and should be a contrasting color. Tie the thread with a square knot (see page 27) so the beads form a ring. This will be the top of the ornament.

Continuing with the same thread that is attached to the ring of beads, string on 11 sets of the following: 5 bridge beads and 1 shared bead. Leave off the shared bead in the last set. Continue working up and down the netting until you have worked around the ring. Close the netting and place on the ornament. Connect the shared beads and do peyote stitch to close the bottom, following the instructions for the Easter Egg above. Attach a tassel if desired.

Netted Soap Dispenser

Decorate your Soft Soap™ Dispenser with a netted skirt.

Supplies

Size 11° seed beads, 15 grams (bridge beads)
252 rice beads (bridge beads)
144 4-mm (or 5-mm) beads (shared beads)
Nylon thread (preferably Nymo D)

Follow directions for the Victorian Tulip Pouch with the following changes: For the initial ring, string on 72 seed beads (do not use larger shared beads in the ring). For the netting, use the 4-mm bead as the shared bead and a seed bead, a rice bead, and a seed bead as bridge beads.

For the first vertical row, string on 2 seed beads, *1 4-mm bead, 1 seed bead, 1 rice bead, 1 seed bead.* Repeat from * to * 6 more times. Then add a 4-mm bead and 1 seed bead and go back through the 4-mm bead. Work up and down the rows following the same pattern and connecting the net to the top ring by going through every fourth seed bead and back through the last 2 seed beads and the last 4-mm bead added. Do not close the bottom. Remove the cap from dispenser and slip the net over the opening. Replace cap.

Elizabeth Ofstead

Triangle Netting

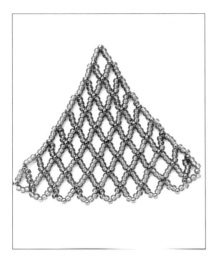

The following instructions are for a basic triangle. Make one, then you will understand how you can vary it to make a larger or smaller triangle. To make the triangle more elongated, use more bridge beads between the shared beads. You will begin at the lower left corner of the triangle and work up and down to the right. For a stiffer triangle, use doubled and well-waxed thread. For a softer triangle use single thread.

Supplies

Size 11° or 14° seed beads

Nylon thread (preferably Nymo D)

1. Thread your needle with a single thread 1½ yd long. String on 1 shared bead and 3 bridge beads 4 times. Go through the first bead toward the tail. Tie the tail to the working thread (Figure 1).

2. Add 3 bridge beads and 1 shared bead twice. Go back through the last 3 bridge beads and 1 shared bead (Figure 2).

3. Add 3 bridge beads, 1 shared bead, and 3 bridge beads. Go through the shared bead in the loop below as shown (Figure 3).

4. Add 3 bridge beads and 1 shared bead twice and 3 bridge beads. Go through the shared bead of the previous set (Figure 4).

Figure 1

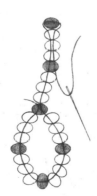

Figure 2

Figure 3

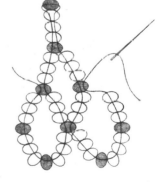

Figure 4

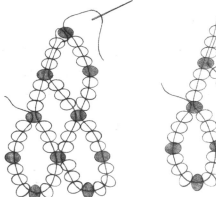

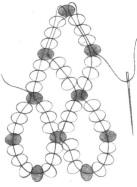

Figure 5 *Figure 6*

5. Add 3 bridge beads, 1 shared bead, and 3 bridge beads. Go through the shared bead at the tip (Figure 5).

If you wish to make the triangle larger, add another spike by repeating Step 2 and working back down and then up the side of the triangle.

When the triangle is the desired height, continue with the next step.

6. Turn and go back through the last 3 bridge beads and 1 shared bead (Figure 6).

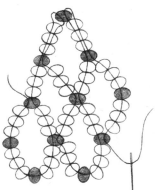

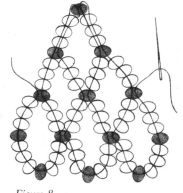

Figure 7 *Figure 8*

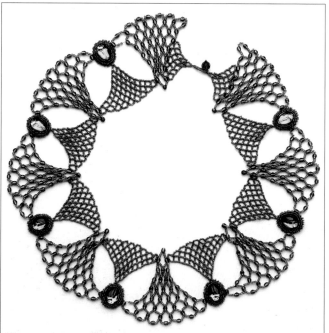

Jane Langenback

7. Add 3 bridge beads, 1 shared bead, and 3 bridge beads. Working down the triangle, go through the next shared bead as shown (Figure 7).

8. Add 3 bridge beads and 1 shared bead twice and 3 bridge beads. Go through the shared bead of the previous set (Figure 8).

Variation 1

If you would like to use the triangle as a leaf, add a stem after Step 5. Add 3 bridge beads and 1 shared bead twice then, skipping the last bead, go back through all the beads just added, the shared bead at the tip, and the next 3 bridge beads and 1 shared bead.

Variaton 1

Variation 2

To shape the triangle, go through all the shared beads only along the base of the triangle and pull tight to gather. Knot thread and weave in the tail.

Variaton 2

Variation 3

For a necklace of triangles, make several and join them at the shared bead on an outer edge of the triangle.

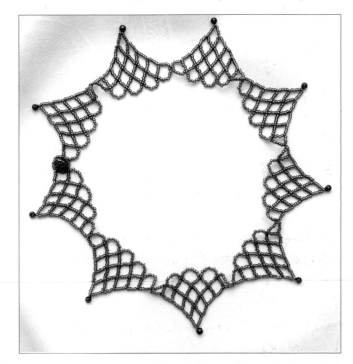

Ann Gilbert

• • • • • •

My Secret Garden Charm Bag

My Secret Garden Charm Bag is a delightful little pouch to wear around your neck. It is made in a tube of three-bead netting with a flap, which is embellished with flowers and leaves. Charms such as flowers, birds, rabbits, butterflies, bugs, and other garden things may be added outside or kept inside.

Supplies

Size 11° seed beads, 2 hanks or 60 grams in one color and small amounts for flowers and leaves

Nylon thread (preferably Nymo D)

Cardboard tube from a toilet paper roll

Adhesive tape

Netted Beadwork for the Body of the Bag

This bag is worked around a cardboard tube. String on 4" of seed beads in groups of 4 at a time (you will need a multiple of 4). Tie them into a ring using a square knot (see page 27) and leaving a 6" tail which will be used later to attach the Lace Chain.

Cut the cardboard tube lengthwise and roll it to fit inside the ring of beads so that the beads are tight against the tube. Secure the tube with tape so that it retains this size.

Row 1: Add 3 beads and pass the needle into the fourth bead from the knot, forming a loop.

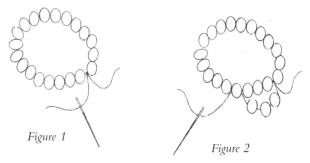

Figure 1

Figure 2

To simplify these illustrations, fewer beads than called for are shown.

Continue adding 3 beads and going into the fourth bead until you return to the first bead that your thread exited at the beginning of this row. Go through this bead (Figure 3, arrow #1). Next, go through the first 2 beads of the first loop formed in this row (Figure 3, note arrows #2 and #3). This is called the "jump" and positions your thread to work the next row.

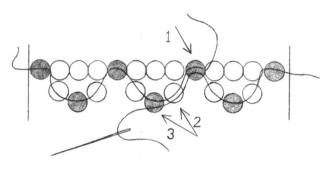

Figure 3

Row 2: Add 3 beads and go into the middle bead of the next loop (Figure 4). Work around the tube. At the end of the row, go into the center bead of the next and last loop, then down through 2 beads so that your thread is exiting the center bead in that loop (the "jump" to the next row).

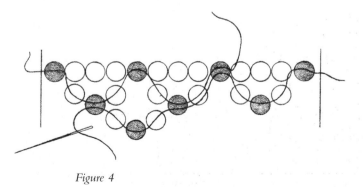

Figure 4

Continue working the netting until the tube is 2¾" long. Knot the thread and weave in the tail.

Making the Flap

Remove the netting from the tube. Anchor a new 1½ yd length of thread so that it is coming out of the center bead of a loop in the top row. Work flat netting stitch (Figure 5) across half of 1 edge of the tube, forming a flat piece. Add 3 beads and pass your needle through the center bead of the next loop.

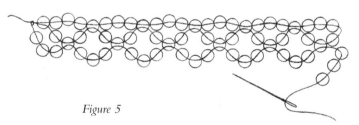

Figure 5

At the end of each row (now working in the opposite direction), add 3 beads, and go back into the middle bead of the last loop formed. Work the flap in this manner for 1¼". Knot the thread and weave in the tail.

Flowers and Leaves

Following instructions on pages 41–46, make 3 or 4 flowers and 12 to 15 leaves of various sizes.

Sew leaves to the flap and lower corner of the bag, then attach flowers. You may wish to have leaves and flowers climb up the lace chain as well.

Closing the Bottom of the Bag

Anchor a new 1½ yd length of thread so it is exiting a center bead in a loop on the front. Then go through the center bead of a loop on the back side, then one on the front side, until you have closed off the bottom.

Chain Support

Make a Lace Chain 24" long and attach it to the sides of the bag at the top using tails from beginning ring and lace chain.

Rose Hamerlinck

Double Layer Netted Bracelet

This bracelet is made with two layers of netted beadwork. The second layer is added after the first layer is completed and is woven over and under the bridge beads of the first layer. The bracelet is worked back and forth across the width. (It may also be worked across the length, which results in a firmer edge.) Take time to explore this technique by varying the pattern of bridge beads. My thanks go to Ann Gilbert for recreating this technique from a round collar I purchased in Hungary in 1990.

Supplies

Seed beads: 60 grams in a light color (L), 20 grams in a dark color (D)
Nylon thread (preferably Nymo D) to match the beads
2 or 3 small buttons

Thread a needle with a single thread 3 yd long. Tie one D in the middle of the thread leaving a 1½ yd tail, which will be used for the second layer of netting.

Step 1 (Row 1): Add 2L and 1D 7 times (Figure 1). The tail indicates the left side of your work.

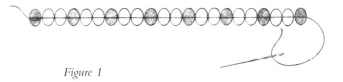

Figure 1

Step 2 (Row 2): Add 3L, 1D, and 3L. Go back through the fourth D going toward the tail (Figure 2).

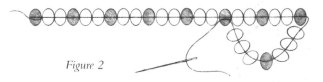

Figure 2

Step 3 (Row 3): Add 3L, 1D, and 3L and, skip 1D, and go into the next D to the left in the previous row. Repeat this step once more (Figure 3).

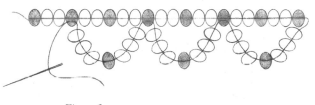

Figure 3

Step 12 (Finishing Row): With the remaining thread tail, work one-and-two drop peyote across the row as follows. From where your threads are knotted together, add 1D and go through the next two L to the left (Figure 12). Repeat across the row. Next row: Add 2L and go into the D in the previous row. Repeat across the row.

Note: Illustrations show only four rows—your piece will be longer.

Add two rows of peyote (see page 59) to the beginning row if desired.

Add buttons and loops for the closure.

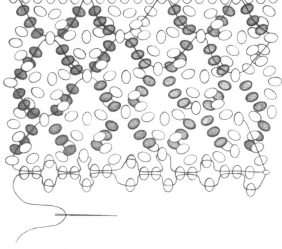

Figure 12

Bonnie Voelker

• • • • • •

Multi-Strand Necklace with Netted Tube

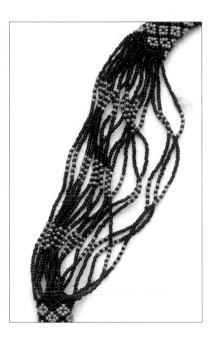

This necklace is made with four short netted tubes that are connected with strands of seed and other beads such as crystals, size 5° triangle beads or size 6° seed beads. The closure is a loop and bead or button. Use the Diamond Pattern provided or you may make your own pattern using the blank graph. In the pattern L is light and D is dark.

Supplies For a 28–29" Necklace*

Seed beads: 50 grams light (L, accent); 75 grams dark (D, main). Use very uniformly sized beads!

336 3-mm round facetted beads, size 6° seed beads, or size 5° triangle beads

Nylon thread (preferably Nymo D)

Button or 10 mm bead

Adhesive tape

approximate length depending on bead size

Making the Tube

With 3 yd of thread in your needle, bring the ends together and wax so strands adhere to each other.

Row 1: String on 32D beads. Tie thread to tails with a square knot to form a ring. Work the tube in your hands or roll a piece of paper about 4 × 5" and slip it inside the ring, letting it expand to fit the ring. Tape the tube to so that it holds its shape.

Row 2: *Pick up 3D. Go into the fourth bead on the beginning ring (Figure 1).

Pick up 1D, 1L, 1D. Go into the fourth bead along the ring* (Figure 2).

Figure 1

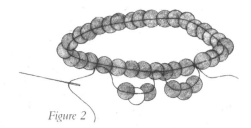

Figure 2

Repeat from * to * 3 more times. Go through the first 2 beads of this row so that your needle is coming out of the middle bead of the first set of 3 in this row (Figure 3).

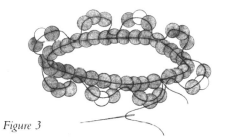

Figure 3

Continue to work the remaining rows of the pattern as indicated in the pattern below. Make 4 tubes. Tie off ends and weave in tails.

Diamonds with Two Colors

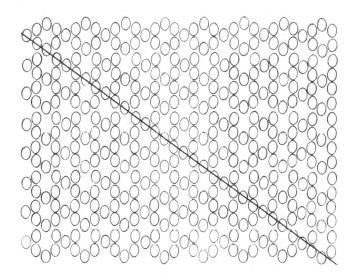

Design your own color pattern with this grid.

Row 1:	32D	
Row 2:	DDD	DLD
Row 3:	DLL	LLD
Row 4:	LLL	DLD
Row 5:	DLL	LLD
Row 6:	LLL	DLD
Row 7:	DLL	LLD
Row 8:	LLL	DLD
Row 9:	DLL	LLD
Row 10:	LLL	DLD
Row 11:	DLL	LLD
Row 12:	LLL	DLD
Row 13:	DLL	LLD
Row 14:	LLL	DDD
Row 15:	32D	
Row 16:	32D	

The diagonal line indicates where a new row begins.

Adding the Closure

With 1 yd of thread in your needle, bring ends together, knot, and melt. Pass needle through 3 to 4 beads along one edge so that it is coming out of a center bead in a loop. Add 10 beads, then add enough beads to form a loop around your button or bead closure. Go back through the last bead of the first 10. Add 9 more beads and go into a bead on the opposite side of the tube. Go back through all these beads at least 2 more times. Knot thread between the last 2 beads. Weave in the tail. Add your button or bead to the other side in a similar manner (Figure 4).

Adding the Strands

With 3 yd of thread in beading needle, bring ends together, knot, and melt. Pass thread through several beads so that it comes out of a center bead of a loop in the bottom of the first tube (the one with the loop side of the closure). See Figure 5.

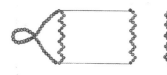

Figure 4

Figure 5

Rose Hamerlinck

Bonnie Voelker

Add beads as follows: 18D, (1L, 1D) 4 times, 1L, 18D, (1L, 1D) 4 times, 1L, 18D, (1L, 1D) 4 times, 1L, 18D.

Go into the center bead of a loop in the next tube. Knot between the beads (see page 27). Repeat pattern for strand. Go into the center bead of the next loop in the first tube. Knot between the beads. Continue back and forth until there are 16 strands.

Connect the last tube (the one with the button side of the closure) and the second last tube in the same way.

Adding the Center Strands

Connect the center strands between the second and third tubes using the following pattern:

18D, (1L, 1D) 4 times, 1L, 18D, (1L, 1 3-mm) 5 times, 1L, 18D, (1L, 1 3 mm) 11 times, 1L, 18D, (1L, 1 3 mm) 5 times, 1L, 18D, (1L, 1D) 4 times, 1 L, 18D.

For a longer necklace, use 6 tubes instead of 4 and adjust length of strands as desired.

White Dots Pattern (B = black, W = white)

Row 1: 32 B

Rows 2–14: BWB

Rows 15 and 16: 32 B

• • • • • •

Rose Bowl Netted Bead Necklace

For this necklace, netting is worked on the bead with the thread passing through the hole of the bead at the end of each row. A small amount of thread will show above and below the netted beads, but this thread will not show when they are strung because the alternating beads will nestle into this space and cover the threads. The netting is worked on a 10-mm wooden bead with size 14° seed beads or on a 14-mm bead with size 11° seed beads. Thanks to Liz Ofstead for recreating this technique from a string of netted beads I found at the Rose Bowl Flea Market in Pasadena, California.

Supplies for each bead

10-mm wooden bead

Size 14° seed beads in four colors, A, B, C, and D

Nylon thread (preferably Nymo D)

1. With 1 yd and leaving a 4" tail to weave in later, tie thread to wooden bead with a square knot (see page 27). Position the knot at the edge of the hole at the top of the bead. Hold the wooden bead with your thumb and forefinger. Use your middle finger to hold the tension

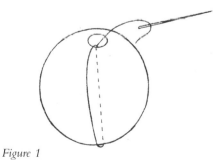

Figure 1

2. String on 1A, 3B, 3C, 3B, 1A.

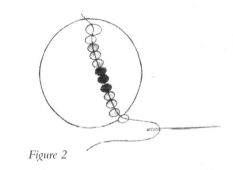

Figure 2

3. Pass working thread through the hole of the wooden bead and tie thread to tail. The knot should sit right above the netting beads.

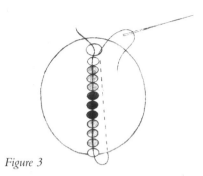

Figure 3

4. Go through the first A bead.

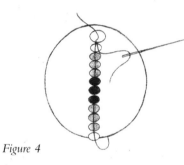

Figure 4

5. Add 3B and 1C. Go through the middle C of the previous row.

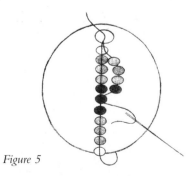

Figure 5

6. Add 1C and 3B and go through the bottom A bead of the previous row, then through the wooden bead.

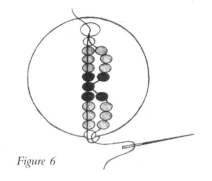

Figure 6

Elizabeth Ofstead

7. Continue attaching the netting beads to the wooden bead following the rows shown in Figure 7 beginning with Row 3. Go through the wooden bead at the end of each row and continue until you have repeated the 6-row pattern a total of 5 times.

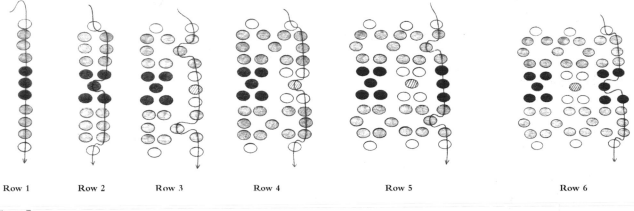

| Row 1 | Row 2 | Row 3 | Row 4 | Row 5 | Row 6 |

Figure 7

8. Lace the ending edge to the beginning edge as shown, adding the new beads that are shown in bold outline (Figure 8).

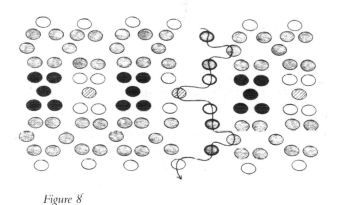

Figure 8

• • • • • •

Bead Collector's Necklace

This necklace is for the bead collector who must have one of each she sees, but then isn't sure what to do with them! The necklace has from five to seven strands of beads varying in size from seed beads to 10 mm beads. The strands are randomly connected, resulting in loose netting, which shows off a variety of beads. Select a color palette of one to three colors with a variety of bead shapes, finishes, and sizes not larger than 14 mm. The necklace may be made either mid-chest length, which is about twenty-six inches, or shorter so that it lies just below the collarbone, about eighteen or nineteen inches.

The inspiration for this necklace comes from one I purchased in the early 1990s when I had just begun to be aware of beads. I was absolutely smitten with it and recall going back to the shop several times to look at it before I finally purchased it with birthday money from my mother-in-law. Later, I was told it was designed by Pat Smiley, a California artist, who has since moved on to other media, especially leather. The design is used here with her permission.

Supplies

All beads should be in a palette of 2 or 3 related colors.
8 to 10 mm beads, about 25 to 30
4 to 6 mm beads, about 40 to 50
3 mm beads or size 6° to 8° seed beads, about 150
Size 11° seed beads in 2 colors, about 30 grams total
Nylon thread (preferably Nymo D)
Multi-strand clasp
Beading needles, size 10 (2)
Foam core board, 2 pieces ¼" thick: one 12 × 15" and one 6 × 10"

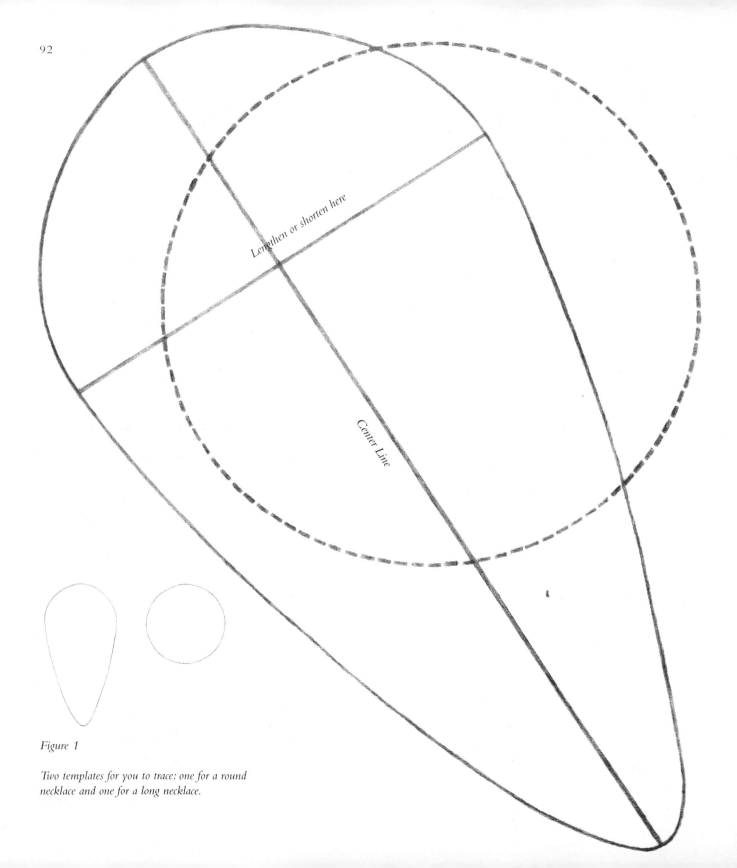

Lengthen or shorten here

Center Line

Figure 1

*Two templates for you to trace: one for a round
necklace and one for a long necklace.*

Making a Template

For a long necklace, cut a piece of foam core board in an inverted teardrop shape 9¾" long and 5" wide. For a round necklace, cut a round template 5½" in diameter. Glue the template to another piece of foam core board that is 9 × 12". You will work around this form to shape the necklace.

The long template is designed for a 26" necklace. The round template is for an 18" necklace, which lies just below the collarbone. Trace the template on ¼" foam core board, cut the shape out, and glue it to another piece of foam core board 9 × 12" using tacky glue. Position template in the center of the board, 1½" from the top edge. Mark center line.

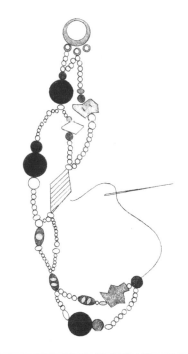

Attaching the Clasp

Pin or tape a clasp at the center top of the template. With waxed Nymo D thread bring the ends together, knot, and singe the end of the thread. Use a lark's head knot to anchor the cord to the clasp (see page 99). Pass the needle through a hole in one side of the clasp nearest the template, pulling the thread so that the knot is 1" from the clasp. Separate the two strands between the clasp and the knot and pass the needle between the strands (Figure 2). Pull tight so that the knot is close to the clasp.

Figure 2

Bonnie Voelker

Begin Stringing

The first strand of the net will lay closest to the edge of the template. String on about 1" to 1½" of seed beads alternating with very small beads (3 to 4 mm) for the first 4" to 5". Continuing with the seed beads, gradually add larger beads with smaller beads on each side until you reach the center. Put an 8 to 10 mm bead at the center. Work your way back up along the other side of the template with a similar pattern of beads until you reach the clasp.

Go through the clasp hole, then back through the last bead. Begin the second strand. String on about ½" of seed beads, a small bead, and ½" of seed beads (approximately) or enough to reach the first small bead. Go through it, beginning to form netting. String on 1" of seed beads, then a few small beads and another 1" or so of seed beads. Go through the next small bead. Continue stringing beads and connecting them to existing beads, gradually increasing the size of the shared beads and placing the most important beads in the lower middle area. Arrange beads so they lay flat next to each other, fitting like a jig-saw puzzle.

Adding New Thread

Add new thread in the middle of a strand, not near the end. Leave the old needle on the thread and thread a new needle with a double overhand knot in the end (singe knot). Pass the new needle through the last 4 to 6 beads just strung so that both needles are coming out of the same bead. (Be sure the knot anchors inside a bead.) Tie the old and new threads together in a square knot (see page 27). String more beads on the new thread. Later bring the old thread through several beads and clip the excess. Apply clear nail polish to the knot.

Finishing

When you reach the clasp after stringing the last strand, go through it, then back through 2 beads and tie 2 half-hitch knots around the thread between the beads (see page 27). Go through a few more beads and repeat. Apply clear nail polish to the knots.

Bonnie Voelker

• • • • • •

Sea Moss Necklace

The Sea Moss Necklace begins with a "backbone" strand of beads, which supports a glass pendant. These beads are usually size 6° (or "E") beads or similar beads about 4 mm in diameter with generous holes that can accommodate a heavier cord as well as several other strands of thread. (Stone beads are not recommended because their holes are often small.) To this backbone strand three or four rows of seed bead loops are added, then strands of seed beads are woven in and out, back and forth through these loops. These strands may be accented with chips or larger beads up to about 6 to 8 mm. The piece is worked on a template.

Supplies

Glass pendant, approximately 1–2" by 2–3"

Seed beads in several colors related to your pendant

Miscellaneous small beads up to 8 mm, stone chips, size 6 or 8 beads, rondelles, etc.

Multi-strand clasp (3 or 4 holes)

Stringing cord, size F

Nymo D from a spool (not a bobbin)

Beading needles, size 10 or 12 (2)

Foam core board, 2 pieces ¼" thick: one 12 × 15" and one 6 × 10"

Tacky glue

Straight pins and clear (not frosted) transparent tape

Small dish for scooping beads (4 × 4 × ¾–1" deep)

Making the Template

Using the 6 × 10" piece of foam core board, draw and cut out the long template shown on page 92. This template will produce a necklace about 26" long. Lengthen or shorten where indicated if desired. Mark the vertical center line. Glue the template to the second piece of foam core board, centering it on the board 1½" from the top. Use tacky glue for quick drying. This template may be reused for other necklaces.

Stringing the Backbone Strand

Tape your pendant to the template, placing the stringing hole along the edge of the template. Use straight pins to position the clasp on the board at the top centerline. Cut a 2-yd length of Size F stringing cord, thread the needle, and bring the two ends together and make a double overhand knot. Clip the tail 1/16" from the knot and melt the knot. Make sure the knot is secure by pulling on it. To make a harness to guide the cord through the beads, thread a beading needle with 6" of Nymo thread, bring ends together, and knot with a square knot (Figure 1). (Think of this loop of thread as the eye of a needle.) Pass the stringing cord through the loop. Bring the ends of the stringing cord together and knot with an overhand knot. Clip tail and melt the knot slightly. Test the knot to be sure it is secure by firmly pulling the strands of stringing cord apart.

Anchoring the Cord to the Clasp

Use a lark's head knot to anchor the cord to the clasp. Pass the loop of the cord through the hole of the clasp

Thread Harness

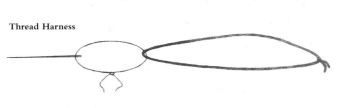

Figure 1

nearest the template, then bring the other end through the loop just formed.

String on backbone beads to reach the pendant, go through the pendant and string more backbone beads to reach the other side of the clasp. Go through the clasp and back through first bead and tie a half-hitch knot around the thread and between the beads (see page 27). Go through 2 beads and tie another knot. Bring the thread through 3 more beads and clip. Apply clear nail polish to all knots.

Attaching Thread to Clasp

Thread a beading needle with 3 to 4 yd of Nymo D thread and bring the ends together. Wax it well so that the strands stick together. This is important because it keeps the thread from tangling, the beads from slipping, and the thread from showing. Knot the ends to-

Lark's Head Knot

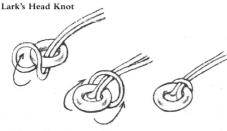

Figure 2

gether with an overhand knot. Clip excess thread $\frac{1}{16}$" from the knot and melt. Attach thread to the middle hole of the clasp using the lark's head knot (Figure 2). Give it a firm tug!

Adding New Thread

When you have about 4" of thread left, leave the needle on the thread. Thread a second beading needle as above, bring the ends together, wax the thread and put an overhand knot in the end. Clip excess and melt. Bring the second needle through the last inch of beads so that it comes out of the same bead in the same direction as the first thread. Tie the first thread and the second thread together with a square knot. Apply clear nail polish to the knot. After more beads have been strung, thread the remaining end of the first thread through these beads and clip the excess.

Stringing Beads

String the beads with the scooping method (see page 55). Place a generous amount of seed beads in a small dish and mound them up in one corner. Hold the needle between your thumb and middle finger and scoop beads from the dish with a slight upward motion. Aim your needle for the middle of the pile where the needle is likely to catch a bead, not along the bottom where beads are likely to be lying with their holes vertical. You should be able to fill a 2" beading needle in 3 or 4 scoops.

String about $1\frac{1}{2}$" of beads and go through the fourth or fifth bead from the clasp. Continue around the backbone string in this way until you have a series

Loop Rows

Figure 3

of loops formed (see Figure 3). When you come to the pendant, pass your needle through it. **Note:** *Be careful here to check the size of the hole in your pendant. If it is large and the seed beads might slip through, go through the last backbone bead right before the pendant and the first one coming out of the pendant hole.* Continue stringing loops up to the clasp. Go through the clasp and then back through 2 or 3 of the beads just strung. Now work around the necklace with a new color in the opposite direction.

Make 2 or 3 more sets of loops in this way, going into a different backbone bead on each round. Each set can be the same or different color. A few silver-lined beads will add sparkle. Transparent beads will lighten the feel of the piece. As you string some loops you may wish to begin adding small beads, chips, or

rondelles within the loop. These add fullness and texture.

Interweaving

With 3 or 4 sets of loops in place, you can begin interweaving. Continue with the same thread. When you come out of the clasp, go through the last few beads strung, then string on a needle full of beads and push them all the way to the end of the thread near the necklace. Randomly weave the thread in and out of the loops going back and forth and up and down. If you only go back and forth, laying round after round on top of each other, you will have lines of color which meander snakelike across the top of your piece rather than an integrated, intertwined appearance. As you string, add a small bead or stone chip every few inches.

At the point where a needleful of beads ends, pass your needle through whatever bead your needle happens to be near to anchor the strand. String on more beads, weave in and out, up and down, and anchor again in the nearest bead. After 3 or 4 rounds have been done this way, your necklace will begin to take on the mossy rope-like appearance. Do as many rounds as you wish until you achieve the desired look and size. Be careful not to overpower your pendant, however. When you have 8 to 10 strands interwoven, tie off your thread just as you did with the end of the cord on the first strand of backbone beads.

A variety of looks can be achieved by the way your interweaving is done. Using smaller loops in the beginning results in a tighter, narrower rope. Large loops result in a less dense, more open look.

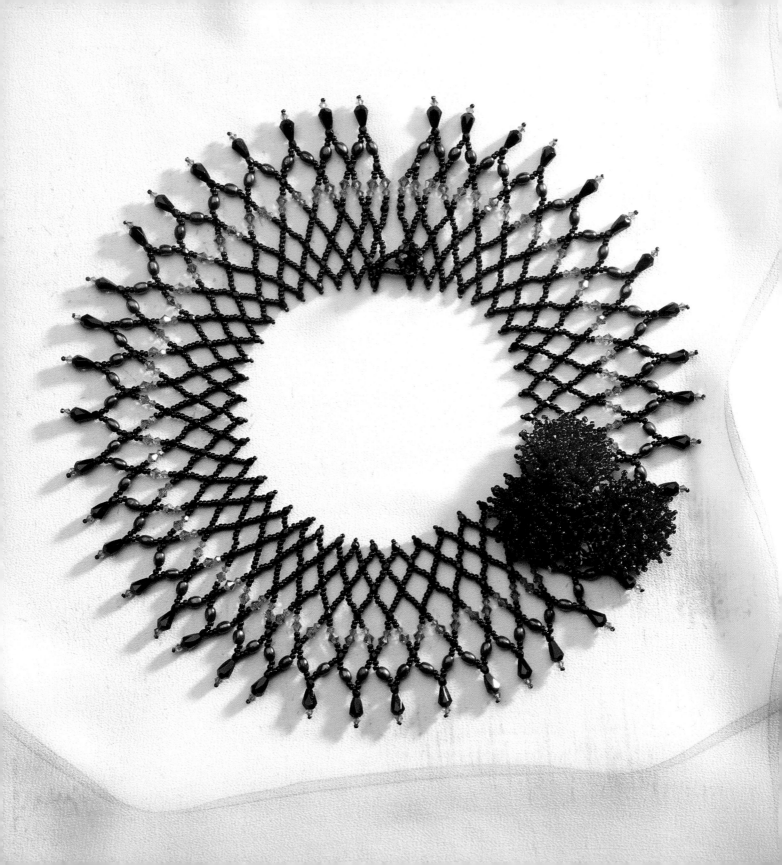

Crystal Collar

This elegant netted collar combines the sparkle of crystals with the luxury of pearls for a beautiful contrast of texture. The collar is somewhat elastic due to the method of construction, making it comfortable to wear. Add three Pom-pom Flowers (see page 41) for an accent. The piece is worked with double thread for durability. Abbreviations for each type of bead are shown in parentheses in the supply list.

Supplies

328 3-mm firepolish crystals (3-fpc)

123 3-mm Swarovski bicone crystals (3-bc)

123 4-mm Swarovski bicone crystals (4-bc)

5 grams Size 14° seed beads (14-sb)

25 grams Size 11° seed beads (11-sb)

82 seed pearls (prl)

41 5 × 7-mm firepolish crystal teardrops with vertical hole (drop)

Nylon thread (preferably Nymo D)

Composition wax (the sticky kind)

See Pom-pom Flower (page 41) for additional flower supplies

 3-mm-fpc

3-mm-bc

4-mm-bc

Size 14°-sb

 Size 11°-sb

seed pearls-prl

 5 × 7-mm -drop

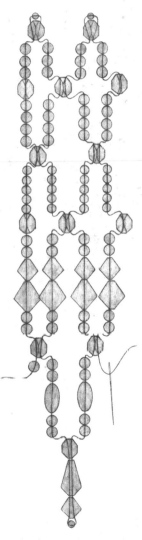

1. Thread needle with a 3-yd length of thread, bring ends together and wax so the strands adhere to each other. Add a stopper bead 3" from the end (add bead and go through it again in the same direction).

2. Add 1 3-fpc, 2 11-sb, 1 4-bc, 1 3-bc, 2 11-sb, 1 3-fpc, 5 11-sb, 1 3-fpc, 4 11-sb, 1 3-fpc, 3 11-sb, 1 3-fpc, 1 14-sb. Go back through (BT) 1 3-fpc.

Add 3 11-sb, 1 3-fpc, 4 11-sb. Go through 1 3-fpc in the previous row.

Add 5 11-sb, 1 3-fpc, 2 11-sb, 1 3-bc, 1 4-bc, 2 11-sb. Go through 1 3-fpc in the previous row. Remove stopper bead and tie working thread to tail.

3. Add 2 11-sb, 1 prl, 2 11-sb, 1 3-fpc, 1 drop, 1 3-bc, 1 14-sb. BT 1 3-bc, 1 drop, and 1 3-fpc.

Add 2 11-sb, 1 prl, 2 11-sb, 1 3-fpc, 2 11-sb, 1 4-bc, 1 3-bc, 2 11-sb. Go through 1 3-fpc in the previous row.

Add 5 11-sb, 1 3-fpc, 4 11-sb. Go through 1 3-fpc in previous row.

Add 3 11-sb, 1 3-fpc, 1 14-sb. BT 1 3-fpc.

Add 3 11-sb, 1 3-fpc, 4 11-sb. Go through 1 3-fpc in the previous row.

Add 5 11-db, 1 3-fpc, 2 11-sb, 1 3-bc, 1 4-bc, 2 11-sb. Go through 1 3-fpc in the previous row.

Repeat Step 3 until there are 41 (or desired number) picots across the top.

4. Knot thread between beads and weave in the tails at the beginning and end.

5. For the clasp, attach an Easy Netted Bead (see page 35) to the second 3-fpc from the beginning edge and a loop of beads to fit around it to the second 3-fpc from the ending edge. 6. Make three Pom-pom Flowers and sew to the necklace about 1½–2" to the right of the necklace center.

Gallery of Netted Beadwork

Diane Fitzgerald
Minneapolis, Minnesota
Teal with Crystals
8½"L, closed

Diane Fitzgerald
Minneapolis, Minnesota
Half Moon Bag and Earrings
Bag: 4"W × 17"L with fringe
Earrings: 1"W × 2½"L

Bonnie Voelker
North St. Paul, Minnesota
Red Necklace with Fringe
18½"L with fringe

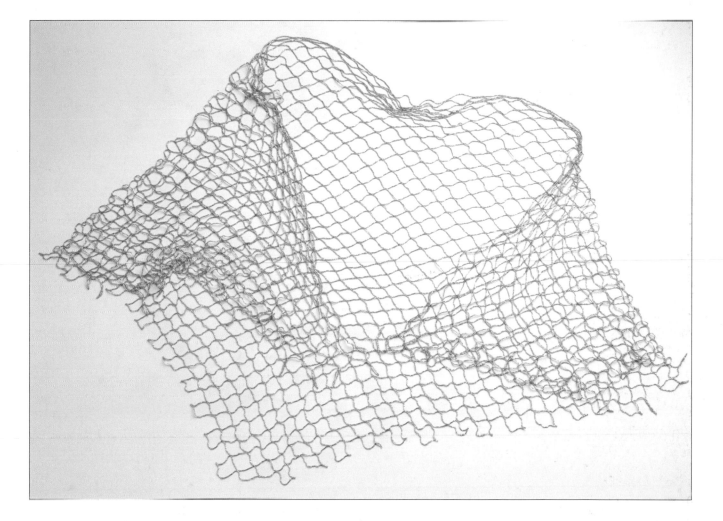

Bonnie Voelker
North St. Paul, Minnesota
Golden Shawl
62"W × 32"L

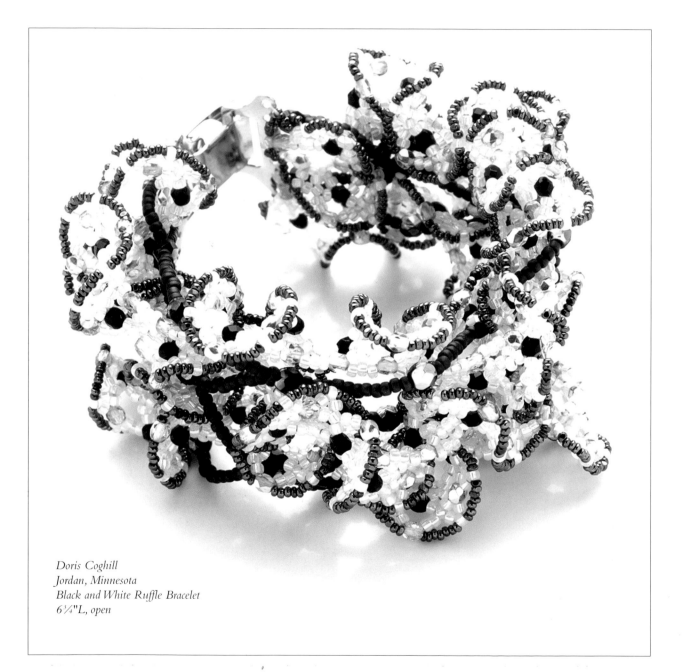

Doris Coghill
Jordan, Minnesota
Black and White Ruffle Bracelet
6¼"L, open

Ann Gilbert
Bloomington, Minnesota
Three Fish and a Worm
Fish: from 1¼" to 3¼"W × 4¼" to 6½"L
Worm: 7"L

Bill Jula
Carnegie, Pennsylvania
Lemko-style Collar
13¾" across with fringe, closed

Bill Jula
Carnegie, Pennsylvania
Lemko-style Collar
12½" across with fringe, closed

Suzanne Golden
New York, New York
Tube Bracelets
Approximately 4⅞" diameter

Maria Rypan
Toronto, Ontario
Sedona Kelim
3½"W at base × 16½"L with fringe

Donna Lish
Clinton, New Jersey
Currents and Whirl
10" and 15" diameters

Kathleen Lynam
Franklin, Tennessee
Punch
A Pop-up Doll
14¼"L

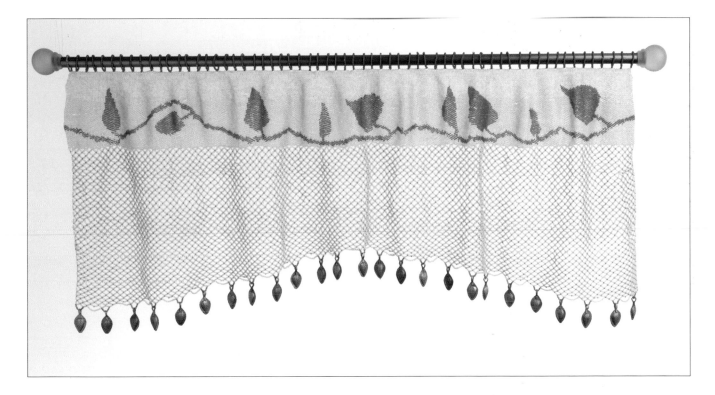

Denise Perreault
Boulder, Colorado
Leaf Me Alone
28"W × 14"L

Roxanne Thoeny
Minneapolis, Minnesota
Lamp Cover with Fringe and Leaves
10½"W × 8½"H

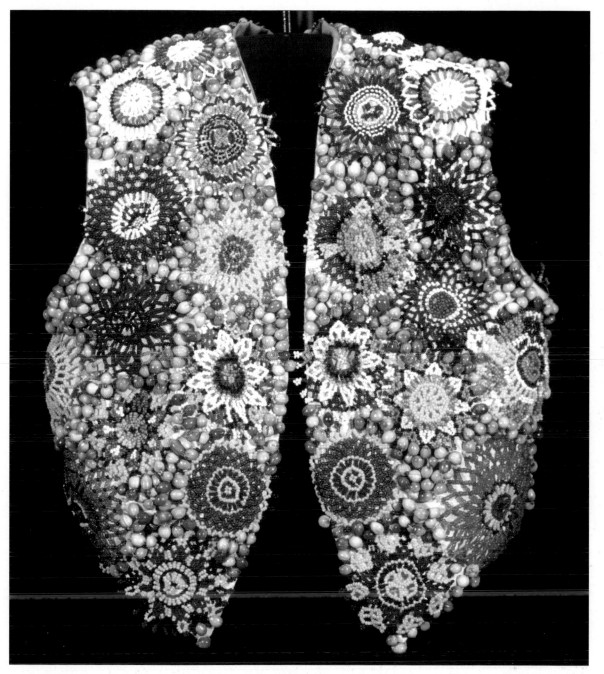

Leslie Pina
Pepper Pike, Ohio
Vest Embellished with African Coasters
Size small

Elizabeth Gourley
Ventura, California
Vertical Netted Necklace
4¾"L

Bibliography

Beads: Sarawak Museum Occasional Paper No. 2. Kuching, Sarawak: Lee Ming Press, 1978.

Chee, Eng-Lee Seok. *Festive Expressions: Nonya Beadwork and Embroidery.* Singapore: National Museum, 1989.

Davis, Jane. *Bead Netted Patterns.* Ventura, California: Davis Designs Press, 1999.

Glassman, Judith. *Step by Step Beadcraft.* New York: Golden Press, 1974.

Goodhue, Horace. *Indian Beadweaving Patterns.* St. Paul, Minnesota: Bead-Craft, 1984.

Grainger, Barbara L. *Dimesional Flowers, Leaves and Vines.* Oregon City, Oregon: Barbara L. Grainger Enterprises, 2000.

Hansen, Keld. *Perler i Gronland.* Copenhagen: National Museum, 1979.

Harte, Mary Ellen. *A Treasury of Beaded Jewelry: Bead Stringing Patterns for All Ages.* Eagle's View Publishing, 1999.

Hector, Valerie. "Pretty Panels, Potent Images: Introducing Dayak Beadwork." *Bead & Button,* Issue #49, June 2002, pp. 16–20

Holm, Edith. *Glasperlen.* Munich: Verlag Georg D. W. Callwey, 1984.

Jones, Mrs. C. S, and Henry T. Williams. *Ladies Fancy Work.* New York: Henry T. Williams, 1876.

Lorenz, Cheryl. "Ecuadorian Bead Weaving." *Bead & Button,* Issue #49, June 2002, pp. 88–92

Makela, Merry. *The Magic of Beaded Spherical Nets.* College Station, Texas: Honey Beads Press, 1996.

Martin, Celia. "Holiday Elegance." *Bead & Button,* December, 2000, pp. 45–46.

Meng, Ho Wing. *Straits Chinese Beadwork and Embroidery: A Collector's Guide.* Singapore: Times Books International, 1987.

Munan, Heidi. *Sarawak Crafts: Methods, Materials and Motifs.* Singapore: Oxford University Press, 1989, pp. 56–64.

Nanavati, J. M. *The Embroidery and Beadwork of Kutch and Saurashtra.* Gujarat, India: Government Press and Stationery Department, Baroda, for the Department of Archaeology, Government of Gujarat, India, 1966.

Nathanson, Virginia. *The Pearl and Bead Boutique Book.* Great Neck, New York: The Hearthside Press Inc. Publishers, 1972, pp. 54–64).

Osborne, Jenna. "Berry Patch Necklace." *Jewelry Crafts* magazine, April 2002, pp. 17–18.

Rypan, Maria. *Overview of Unkranian Beadwork. Toronto: Rypan Designs, 2002.*

——. Netted Mesh Collars: *Lesson No. 1.* Toronto: Rypan Designs, 2002.

——. *Netted Jagged Mesh: Lesson No. 2.* Toronto: Rypan Designs, 2002.

——. *Assorted Beadwork: Lesson No. 1.* Toronto: Rypan Designs, 2002.

Scott, Joyce. *Fearless Beadwork,* 1994.

Sheppard, Mubin. *Living Crafts of Malaysia.* Singapore: International Press, 1978, pp. 86–95.

Siniska, Debbie. *Decorative Beadwork.* New York: Henry Holt & Co., 1995 (pp 49–53 and 79–81).

Star, Vicki. *A Netting Primer.* Vicki Star, 1995.

Vinson, Desiree. *Guide to Beadwork.* Corvallis, Oregon: In Touch Publishing, 1990.

Wells, Carol Wilcox. *Creative Beadweaving.* Asheville, North Carolina: Lark Books, 1996.

White, Mary. *How To Do Beadwork.* New York: Doubleday, Page & Co., 1904.

Index